THE RIDICULOUS MOUNTAINS

The Ridiculous Mountains

*Tales of The Doctor and his friends
among the Highland Hills*

G. J. F. DUTTON

Illustrations by Albert Rusling

DIADEM BOOKS · LONDON

First published in 1984 by
Diadem Books Limited, London
This edition first published 1990

All trade enquiries to:
Hodder and Stoughton
Mill Road, Dunton Green, Sevenoaks, Kent

British Library Cataloguing in Publication Data

Dutton, G. J. F.
  The ridiculous mountains.
  I. Title
  823'.914 [F]   PR6054.U8/

  ISBN 0 906371 38 4

Printed and bound in Great Britain by
Biddles Ltd, Guildford and King's Lynn

Contents

Preface

A word before you step on to the hill with these intrepid mountaineers — on behalf of the exhausted Narrator. He has bravely recounted in this book some of the adventures of himself and his equally hapless companion the Apprentice, when among the summits with the unpredictable Doctor. Because I helped select his tales but was otherwise little involved, he thinks I should briefly introduce them. Very well; but these are my remarks, not his.

The above three characters, with their bizarre but not unfamiliar acquaintances, have by now become fairly well known. Their exploits have been several times anthologised, but mostly first appeared annually in the *Scottish Mountaineering Club Journal*; that indisputably ancient, always informative, usually cantankerous and occasionally excellent publication. Therefore the scene is largely Scotland. This is no disadvantage, mountain problems and protagonists being everywhere similar. An advantage, rather, for the Scottish hills are restricted enough to give these tales all sorts of echoes within their own notably resonant territory; and yet extensive enough to display almost the full horrendous spectrum of today's mountain activity and anti-activity.

So in these pages we wander green-backed over whales in leisurely pursuit of pimples; feast and snore in tent, howff or igloo; and clutch the fiercest *sestissimo grado* of rock or ice. We encounter such ancillary occupations as caving, bird-watching, skiing, sailing, deerstalking, mossgathering and mountain rescue. Dogs, flies, wardens, gamekeepers and police assail us. Landowners, executives and the Armed Forces of the United States of America welcome us to their tables. We could, with due regard for climate, custom and uniform, be in the Alps, the Lakes, California, Wales, Nepal, New Zealand, the Caucasus: anywhere among mountains. The oromaniacal quest (as Norman Collie termed it in the *Journal* quoted above 90 years ago) takes the same sanely irrational course, whatever militant industrialists or industrious militarists surround it. And it separates its devotees into the same mutually exclusive clubs in all places. We hear of two in these pages. One, nineteenth century in origin and eccentricities; one more disposable, and more self-consciously at the cutting edge of climbing technique. To set off our pleasant illusion of Progress in Mountaineering, both are necessary; their careful friction warms the heart.

Arrangement of these tales is not chronological in any sense. Publication dates are noted in the Contents. As evident from the Narrator's own remarks, adventures often occurred in a different order to that of their publication. Some authorities have implied that these adventures never occurred at all. Against that, I myself was sufficiently at hand in several of them to confirm the Narrator's testimony. As for the rest, we have all met with experiences similar enough to support their authenticity. There should be no doubt. However, in a few instances, and as a matter of simple discourtesy, names have been exchanged. And one participant has, on personal demand, been expunged: the Doctor's wife. She appears somewhere below only as a (presumably willing) supplier of curtain material. She refused to allow publication of her own remarks on the usually dishevelled Sunday evening return of her errant spouse. They were always pungent; and invariably prefaced by: 'Well, and what have you been doing today, on your ridiculous mountains?'

G.J.F.D.
1984

1

A Good Clean Break

We coiled the rope. It had been a good route. Warm eastern granite, and now sunburnt heather. The Doctor arranged himself elaborately at full length, head pillowed on arms.

'It *is* a shout,' confirmed the Apprentice, looking up from his last coils.

We listened. A feeble cry, which might once have been 'Help', wandered up from the other, easier, side of the crag. I peered, but saw nothing.

The Doctor reassembled his full height, climbed a convenient protuberance, and inspected the heathery hollow below.

'There! It *is* somebody. Chap lying on a ledge. Some ass fallen off.'

This was one of the Apprentice's best days. He was in excellent form, and swiftly led me down a steep series of slabs to the victim. The Doctor, irritatingly, arrived first, having walked down a heathery rake neither of us had seen.

'Well, and who are you?' asked the Doctor pleasantly, as he took off his jacket, knelt, and rolled up his sleeves.

'I'm the Casualty,' announced the figure, not altogether surprisingly.

'So it seems. Now,' said the Doctor, frisking him professionally, 'have you any pain? Back or limbs?'

'I'm bloody stiff,' remarked the Casualty. 'Been here hours.'

'Of course you'll be stiff. But have you any pain?'

'Only when you poke me like that. Who are *you* anyway?'

We all raised eyebrows. The Doctor adopted his blandest bedside approach, suitable for dealing with irate landowners, lunatics, or the concussed.

'Never mind, laddie. We're here to help. We'll soon get you down.'

'Get *me* down?' remarked the Casualty sarcastically. 'I think you'd better get *them* down.' And he stood up, yawned, hobbled stiffly to one side and, most disconcertingly, proceeded to empty his bladder over the edge of the cliff.

The Doctor was as near nonplussed as I have seen him. His fingers stroked the air; his cuffs — now loose again — fluttered uncertainly. '*Them*? Who are *they*?'

'The Rescue Team,' remarked the Casualty, turning and adjusting his dress. 'They're all stuck. Up there,' he added, jerking his head towards the cliff behind us.

We turned. Some eighty feet up, a collection of cagouled figures fluoresced ashamedly from various unlikely positions. One was clearly upside down, resting on his elbows. All (fortunately) were tied together by a welter of ropes. In reply to our gaze, they mewed in chorus a feeble and obviously highly embarrassed 'Aaa . . . help.'

The Casualty sat on an outcrop and lit a fag. 'I suppose we'll have to go and sort 'em out,' he said. When pressed to describe the nature of his accident, he explained that it was no accident, but just his turn to be Casualty. It was, he further explained, and somewhat belatedly, an Exercise. Training. This was the Pitfoulie Mountain Rescue Team. They came out every weekend, if the weather was fine. A sort of a club. Good fun, and useful.

The Doctor, cheated of his prey, was reluctant to believe all this. 'Concussion,' he confided to us, 'has curious effects. Now I've —'

'Concussion?' broke in the Casualty. 'He got that all right. Same as last time. Always gets it. That's why they're in that mess.' He jerked his fag towards the now silent tableau.

'So there is a real casualty, after all!' exclaimed the Doctor, brightening and rising to his feet. He brushed down his breeches and slipped on his jacket. 'The sooner we fix him up the better.'

'Och, he's all right now, Eck is,' said the Casualty, inhaling and blowing the smoke out again in neat little rings. 'We just drove him back to town. He'll get home in a day or two, like last time. They usually do, with mild concussion,' he informed the Doctor.

Eck, it turned out, was Leader of the Pitfoulie team. He had started it, having apparently discovered a passion for Rescue when a mere boy. His absence accounted for the failure of this particular exercise. The rest of the team — apart from the Casualty, who was experienced enough but, as he explained, had to take his turn as Casualty like anyone else — the rest were not too familiar with complex rope manoeuvres and had gradually fankled themselves into complete stasis.

'But how did Eck get concussion?' demanded the Doctor, still obsessed.

'He fell out of our Land Rover. He always does. He's that eager. He leans out, directing us, as soon as we drive on to the hill. It holds things up. We didn't get started again till 11 o'clock — though we were quicker this time than last.'

So the question resolved itself simply into the four of us releasing the rescue team. We turned ourselves towards the cliff, the Casualty nipping out his fag-end with some regret. Just as we were about to plunge down the heather to the foot of the crag, a line of figures appeared above our bowl, twittering.

'Careful, now! It's an EDGE!' boomed out a rich contralto voice, with more than a brush of five o'clock shadow on it. 'Stop where you are!'

One figure, that of a long thin man in a flapping raincoat, did not stop. He slipped, sat down on his raincoat and began, inexorably, to slither towards the edge of the crag. Our eyes popped. The Doctor smelt game.

'I said STOP, Mr Pilchard! I SAID STOP!'

Mr Pilchard slowed down and, obediently, stopped. A large female figure made towards him and plucked him, raincoat fluttering, back to safety. The excited buzz of conversation resumed.

'It's Mrs Cairnwhapple,' said the Doctor. 'Ursula Major. And that's her ornithological party. A breeding pair was reported here last week.'

Mrs Cairnwhapple, no mean woman, took in the scene at a glance. 'Just as well we STOPPED, friends. There are four foolish people down there who did not stop and who are now In Trouble. They are waiting to be rescued by the experienced mountaineers you see below you.' (Agonised twitchings from the web.) 'A real Rescue Team. We must sit and watch, and pick up some Useful Hints.' She plumped herself down in the heather, her chicks snuggling likewise. She kept a sharp eye on Mr Pilchard, who still exhibited suicidal tendencies.

We may imagine the next hour or so. Sufficient to say that by the time we disentangled the rescue team and took them down to the foot of the crag, a late June sun had mellowed into early evening. And Mrs Cairnwhapple, with a bittern-like boom of delight, had recognised the Doctor and had trodden heavily and decisively down heather and ledge to join us. Her wheepling brood accompanied her, Pilchard suffering minor mishaps on the way. The Apprentice, who had performed daring deeds over the past two hours, was particularly helpful to one admiring and attractive young lady ornithologist. 'That's Ann Scarsoch,' said the Doctor, rejoining me after wearily separating once again two entwined and fluorescent rope-coilers. 'Old Poltivet's daughter. Only yellow plastic soles on her shoes. Flighty piece.'

Mrs Cairnwhapple had caused baskets to be produced and opened; we munched in satisfaction. The Pitfoulie team, though still somewhat subdued, finished first and, with a commendable sense of duty, stretched out their casualty once more and began trussing him up for the carry-down. The Doctor was suggesting we should examine their knots. 'After all, they're doing it on purpose this time.' Behind us in the heather, the Apprentice was teaching La Scarsoch the technique of pressure grips.

Suddenly we froze. Beneath us, up the long slopes of the evening glen, the sunlight heaved with an army of people. Crowd after crowd. The Doctor snatched up his binoculars.

He paled. 'Rescue Teams. Walkie-talkies. Army. Air Force. Police. Navy. Shepherds. Civilians. Dogs. Schoolboys.' We listened. Yes . . . and helicopters.

We hurried over to the Casualty. (The Apprentice was too much engaged to notice.) We asked him what he knew of this invasion. Was it another, but mammoth, Exercise?

The Casualty, with disarming ease, freed his left arm from a splint, and pulled the bandages from his mouth. He sat up and grinned.

'No, it'll be a real one this time. We'll have to join it. They *still* mustn't have come back to that car. Two whole days away, no notification, no sketch of route taken. Must be lost. That lot'll find 'em. Not that they'll want to be found, when they tot up the cost of this little trip.' He complacently stripped off his dressings, rose, and assumed command.

The Doctor and I felt the earth wither. Why, oh why *had* he parked in that car park? Why *had* he bought a parking ticket? Against all our rules. Yet there was still hope . . . What sort of car was it, what number? Did anyone know?

The Casualty frowned. The occasion was rather too important for trivial curiosity. 'A big old German crate. Yes, a Merc.' Number? He had, of course, noted that. He pulled out a grubby bit of paper and read off the Doctor's registration number . . .

That was that. We would share his costs certainly, despite his protestations, but nothing could lessen the blow from the Accident Report in the next *Journal*. Hummel Doddie wrote these Accident Reports, it was rumoured (by all except Hummel Doddie); Hummel Doddie, whose active pen flayed the tomfools that caused unnecessary searches, that caused vast and growing inconvenience to vast and growing mountain-fuls of rescuers (the helicopters nosed above us, attracted by the carrion-beetle orange of the Pitfoulie cagoules); Hummel Doddie would certainly not spare — and rightly not spare — the Doctor, whose views (like those of the Apprentice) on these matters were not the views of the establishment . . .

'Blast it,' said the Doctor. He bravely stood and watched the attackers close in. His pipe remained unlit.

At that moment there was a crack, followed by a scream. We all sprang round. Miss Scarsoch sat up in the heather, white and holding her wrist. The Apprentice stood beside her, rumpled and red. He had been trying to teach the Layback, but clumsy-like . . .

With a glad cry, the Doctor leapt forward and knelt down. He felt the wrist nimbly. He looked up. His eyes brimmed with happiness.

'A Colles, by the Lord. We're saved. A good clean break!'

He issued orders in all directions. The Pitfoulie team, led by their casualty, marched towards him. Behind them rose the dust of advancing myriads, the barking of dogs. The air grew thick with engines and whirring metal, with cries and commands. Miss Scarsoch would doubtless have fainted, had not Mrs Cairnwhapple bellowed encouragement in her ear.

'Stick it, Ann! A little thing like that!'

As the impis approached, their aerials glittering in the setting sun, the Apprentice gloomily held Miss Scarsoch's other hand and thought, like me, of our small brown tents alone in the Upper Corrie. The Doctor thought of them, too, but also of a large empty Mercedes surrounded by cameramen and police officers; and blessed the animal spirits of the young human male.

I could imagine his conversation when he at last got back to his car. The saluting police officers. Himself breezily nonchalant. 'Aye, a nasty business officer, but could have been worse, could have been worse.' 'Verra fortunate you were up there, Doctor.' 'Aye, we're often called upon to render assistance wherever we may be. Inconvenient, but must be done. The Oath, you know, officer, the Oath.' 'Aye, sir, the Oath.' 'Inconvenient to you, too, officer — I expect, ah, I expect you thought I'd got lost or something, with my car here so long?' 'Och, no, sir, no' (deprecatingly). 'One never knows when one may be delayed on this sort of business. One always has to be ready.' 'Oo aye, sir, ye cannae tell, ye cannae tell.' 'Why, I've still some Glen Houlet . . . I'll not risk any more, driving. But yourself — must be fairly tired and cold, officer . . . eh?' 'Och . . . ' Mutual exchange of understanding. We would be saved.

That night, as we packed up our tents, the Doctor showed us the piece of paper he had been scribbling on by torchlight. 'I'm sending it to Hummel Doddie,' he said. 'Old Doddie likes his reports in early, and from those first on the scene. Later on, you know, there could be all sorts of confusion.' His eyes gleamed beneath the midnight sun.

The paper read:

30th JUNE — Ann Scarsoch (19), Scottish, fairly experienced, practising layback with more experienced companion at foot of corrie below Grouse Shoot, Lochnagar, fell her length. Fractured wrist, shock, some exposure. Found and brought down by Pitfoulie M.R. team (acting leader Alec Sprachle). Injuries dressed on spot by doctor climbing nearby. Invaluable assistance given by Army, R.A.F. and R.N. teams, shepherds, police and civilians. Dogs used. Large bodies out, including Mrs Ursula Cairnwhapple, M.B.O.U. Two helicopters broke down but crews rescued by Army, R.A.F. and R.N. teams, shepherds, police and civilians; dogs used. One policeman bitten by dog; injuries dressed on spot by doctor climbing nearby. One civilian, T. Pilchard (41), English, lost on way down; found in hotel bar later.

A considerably shortened version appeared in the subsequent *Journal*.

2

The Craggie

Just on the corner, the wheel came off. Fortunately, it was a right-hand corner and an off-side wheel. I was sitting in the front and saw it appear in the headlamp beams, skipping joyfully in its new freedom. Speechless, I grabbed the Doctor's shoulder, and pointed.

'Ah, a wheel,' he said.

I curled myself up in the old nylon sling which served as safety belt, and watched fascinatedly through the fingers shielding my face.

Imperturbably, we slowed down, bumped along the grass verge and clomped to a halt. The wheel waved us goodbye and leapt into a sitka plantation. The Doctor opened his door and got out.

'Extraordinary. Rear wheel. Never happened before. Handled very well, considering it's i.r.s.' He rummaged in a door pocket, then he went off by torchlight to retrieve the errant accessory.

In grateful obscenity from the back seat the Apprentice voiced his admiration. We both agreed the Doctor was no more nerve-wracking to his passengers on three wheels than on four.

Before he returned, bowling his wheel, we had confirmed that the threads had stripped. We were stuck on a wet Saturday night in late October, halfway to our goal.

Our goal was a kindred club hut below a well-known and easy ridge. We were to scramble up the ridge and down again;

a mere excuse for a spirituous weekend to celebrate the Doctor's achievement and our own survival — for the previous weekend we had taken him up his first V.S. An experience cathartic for us — even for the iron-nerved Apprentice, who as usual led — but apparently much enjoyed by our medical companion. I need not describe it here.

We were stuck. We had no tent, and even the Doctor's old Mercedes could not sleep three when one of them was his own six feet two. We inspected the map.

'Here's the road, the plantation. Ah!' He gave a glad cry, thumped his thigh with the torch. The light went out. 'We're just by Kindraiglet! What luck!'

The luck turned out to be that Kindraiglet was a cottage on his brother-in-law's estate. It was occupied by his brother- -in-law's shepherd. 'An excellent man, MacPhedran. He'll be delighted to put us up. Remarkable luck. And — yes — I'll give you a treat tomorrow.' He chuckled ominously as he wrestled out his rucksack.

Two hours later we were admitted by a jovial MacPhedran. 'Car broke down, just on the road below,' explained the Doctor, dismissing our purgatorial sojourn in drenching 20- foot sitka spruce — the prickliest stage of growth — looking for the Kindraiglet track. ('Can't be far off; know it well; pity these trees are so high; otherwise my torch would easily pick it out.')

We dried, feasted, drank and sang. MacPhedran fiddled with gusto. When I fell asleep the Doctor and he were trying to explain to each other what went wrong with Scott Skinner.

The morning was fine, though cold and dripping. After cooking a late breakfast (MacPhedran was long on the hill) the Doctor referred again to his Treat.

'It was damn good of you to take me up *Constipation* last weekend. I'd never have cared to go alone. Wouldn't have missed it for the world. Remarkable how straightforward those routes are when you rub noses on 'em. Well, here's one for you two. Used to stay here years ago. Always went on The Craggie, as we called it. A jolly nice little climb, quite different from *Constipation*. You'll like the change.'

So it was to be The Craggie. We had brought the minimum of equipment — only a 60-foot line and the odd assortment of ironware inseparable from the Apprentice (he clinked perceptibly even in Daddy McKay's). But we were assured The Craggie would require none of it. 'Used to go on The Craggie by myself — just boots. Balance is all you need — and an eye for a good line.'

He led out of the door. The Apprentice and I, heavy-headed, tried to imagine the amorous rugosities of warm gabbro. We splashed up through the birches.

Disconcertingly soon, he stopped. 'There she is!' he announced. We peered past him at a clearing in the scrub. Out there, moss and slime, so long beneath our feet, reared themselves up to a sheer three hundred evil feet. The upper rim was fanged in black; and black rock gleamed hungrily at us through a thousand green and dripping moustachios.

'Wonderful view from the top,' he said. Then: 'Good Lord, there *she* is!'

'Who now?' asked the Apprentice, sourly. His pallor, I noted, was not all attributable to the night before.

'Why, Aggie. Aggie McHattie. Up there, on the left. The old girl in tweeds. See her? Just by that big wet slab. I *thought* I heard a car early on.'

I found the Apprentice's expression interesting. Then I turned again to the extraordinary sight. The Doctor lowered his Leitz Trinovids and lent them to me. I saw, bang in the middle of the face, a square figure in tweed jacket and skirt, thick socks, nailed shoes, frizzy grey hair and gold spectacles. I saw it standing on a line of slime prising out something from the oozing slab. I saw it lift up the something, examine it, and throw it away. I swore I could hear the 'Pshaw!'

'Hallo,' roared the Doctor. 'Allo, allo, allo,' roared back The Craggie, moistily and throatily. The figure looked round, surveyed us. A clear precise voice.

'Good morning, Doctor. I shan't be long. There's not very much here.' Then it returned to its prising, further along the line of slime.

'Miss Agnes McHattie,' explained the Doctor. 'Remarkable

woman. Famous lichenologist and moss-classifier; not really Ferns, but does take a look or two at the *Ophioglossaceae*. Used to be my leader on lots of expeditions.'

The Apprentice declined the binoculars. Also, he seemed to be having difficulty in swallowing.

We squelched up to the foot of The Craggie. We stopped below a vertical pillar of green treacle. It wet my elbow.

'Central Buttress Direct' said the Doctor. 'A good line on to the Main Face. I'll lead and show you the way at first; although it's obvious enough. Glad I brought trikes; there's a slippery bit near the top.'

He crouched, adopted a curious kind of dog-paddle, and levitated uncannily. He paused and settled on a heap of water-cress or similar vegetation twenty feet up. 'Great to be back again. Lost youth and all that. Come on up, there's acres on this stance.' As he spoke, a large plateful of cress smacked down wetly at my feet. Politely, the Apprentice waved me on. Kindly, he gave me the rope.

'Yes, we may need the rope later on,' the Doctor advised. 'It gets harder in places if you're in vibrams. They're jolly treacherous anywhere off those Trade Routes of yours.'

I agreed. It was impossible even to leave the ground with them. I only succeeded by locking each knee alternately in the soaking groove and spooning heaps of green porridge with both hands to keep me upright. I was not ashamed to take the Doctor's bony grip. I was dragged up, and thankfully clutched a long green stem.

'Ho! Watch that! It's *Lycopodium inundatum*, a mere clubmoss. No root. Dangerous. *Cryptogamma crispa*'s a good handhold. Here's one. Ah, there's *Luzula* — even better. You've got to know your mountains, in a place like this!'

I was in terror lest I should have to offer the Apprentice the rope. But up he came, seaweed in his hair.

The watercress was definitely crowded, and raring to go. So the Doctor continued. I instructed my companion in the deficiencies of *Lycopodium* and the relative security of *Cryptogamma*. He muttered darkly, still clutching the piton with which he had clawed his way up.

The cress hiccupped vertiginously. I grabbed several stems, pressed kneecaps into a Gorgon's head of bryophytes. The Apprentice said he was getting the hell out of here and boldly struck off leftward into a succession of roofs, mere vertical or overhanging rock relatively free of photosynthetic organisms and their less ambitious brethren. He panted and swore. Roots and fragments fell. I patted and reassured my cress.

A clear voice rang out from below and further left.

'What's that boy *doing* up there? He'll fall off. Quite pointless. There's nothing but *Hylocomium squarrosum* in that groove. I looked very carefully this morning.'

The Doctor was above me. I glimpsed his toothed toes projecting from an upper moustache. They dripped past my face.

'It's all right, Aggie,' he said. 'We're just up enjoying ourselves. But can we help *you* at all?'

Silence. Then: 'Ah, Doctor, if you would be good enough to send your Boy down here' (mercifully inarticulate splutters from the left) 'I could use him very well just now.'

My companions are both gentlemen. The Doctor continued gazing at the view. The Apprentice clambered and slithered down to Miss McHattie's line of slime.

She nodded, and beckoned him. 'Carefully, now. Just stand here. Oh, you've got boots. *Rubber* boots. How foolish. Should be nailed. And should be *shoes* — for proper flexion on small ledges. But I expect you've Weak Ankles. That's why most people have to wear boots. You should walk more. Now stand carefully there, and hold on to this loose piece of rock here and this clump of *Cystopteris*. CYSTOPTERIS! Not *Cephalozia!* That's right. Bend a little, for I'm going to have to step on to your back, I'm afraid. We'll never reach that *Stereocaulon* otherwise. Very glad you've come. I have a meeting tonight in Edinburgh, and I really must go down after this.'

The Apprentice described graphically afterwards the weight of the old battleship, and displayed the variegated indentations of triple hobs and muggers trodden across his vertebrae.

She poked away at a shiny clump with her trowel, fretting with annoyance. The Apprentice gingerly let go *Cystopteris,* tapped her shoe and offered up his piton. She tried it. Her comments were punctuated by chipping.

'H'm, useful tool. Better than anything I've brought, for this job, I must say. Where did you get it? *Who?* A most curious name. Never heard of him. A great number of' (continuous chipping) 'odd persons have taken advantage of the recent interest in lichenology. Especially since Toshpatrick-Gilchrist cleaned up all the *Lecidea alpestris* variants on Ben A'an. Winter forms, too. *That* made headlines. Curious name Fifo. An immigrant, no doubt. An opportunist. He won't last, poor fellow. I get all my ironware from Pflanzhanger of Munich. Still, it's very useful' (renewed chipping) 'I particularly like the hole in the handle; one could string them on to one's belt. Very handy. I'll write old Pflanzhanger himself about it. Quite time these continentals caught up on Edinburgh firms.'

Miss McHattie scraped down her spoil, lifted her spectacles, examined it, and nodded approvingly. She handed the Apprentice a mucilaginous clot. 'Hold this, young fellow,' she said '*Stereocaulon* AND *Cerania vermicularis*, an aberrant type.' She hauled at a cord, and a haversack rose from the depths behind her. The Apprentice backed in astonishment. She eyed him severely. 'Be careful, or you'll slip. That would never do. It's the first record west of Clova at this height.' She stuffed the desirable morsels into a small tube, clapped it into her haversack, and began to shuffle rapidly towards a grassy rake. Then she stopped, smiled meaningly, pulled a small flask from a voluminous pocket, poured out a generous capful of spirit and bade the Apprentice quaff. He quaffed, appreciatively. He rubbed his eyes. She screwed the flask back into her tweeds.

'Well, thank you. I expect the Doctor is teaching you to climb. A dangerous pastime, I always think. But the Doctor is an incurable Romantic. He indulges a veritable passion for the more vascular plants. I confess I outgrew the Angiosperms when I was a mere girl; we were positively stuffed with them at school. The Doctor, I fear, is more Byzantine. However, mind you listen to what he tells you, and don't fall off. Goodbye.' And rapidly she handed herself downwards out of sight. Before vanishing, she paused and looked up. 'Goodbye Doctor,' she roared; and the cress trembled.

'Remarkable woman,' mused the Doctor, turning again to the wall. 'Had an entire liverwort subspecies named after her — *Dicronodontium uncinatum McHattii*; should have been a genus — *Agnesia*'. He appeared greatly amused by this, and chucklings punctuated the falling moss.

We assembled beneath the final pitch, a quite vertical water-meadow. Our stance was the usual loose-stoppered and quavering cold-water-bottle. 'This is tricky. We *could* go down, if you like.' Below us the cliff dropped its 250 feet to the bottom boulders — which, characteristically, were the only bare rocks at The Craggie. They leered knowingly. Chorally, we shuddered and said no. 'The rock's quite smooth underneath, but the vegetation's sound as a bell, provided you use the insides of your arms and legs. Don't of course use your feet, or try to kick. A pity you don't wear tweed. Nylon slides off everything. Most unsatisfactory.'

He smiled paternally, dived upwards and swam rapidly out of sight. We had persuaded him to take the 60-foot line, just in case. When it was my turn I got no further than halfway. I trod water breathlessly. Below me a great sodden wig of *Plagiothecium* peeled off and smacked on the anxious upturned face of the Apprentice. He reappeared, spluttering, but still adherent.

'Ha, I told you it was safer than *Constipation,*' cried the Doctor encouragingly, as from a boat, 'if that had been rock, all your helmets wouldn't have stopped it!'

Meanwhile, the current was washing me backwards. Towards the new black shiny rock. I called, almost for help. The Doctor swiftly knotted the line to a stem and threw me down the loose end.

'Might need a fixed rope, first time up,' he agreed.

By grabbing and changing from crawl to butterfly, I reached him on his mouldering rugosity. As I looked up, a wet jelly licked my face. I spat it out.

'Ha, *Hirneola aurticula-judae* — Jew's-ear fungus.' It encircled my stem. The Doctor calmed me.

'No, it doesn't attack the roots. The stem's quite sound low down where the rope is. It's rowan — fine strong safe rooting system — pliable cortex. Now if it had been ash — ' he shook his head expressively. 'Many a good climber's been let down badly by young ash. Fine in an ice-axe. But not on the hoof.'

Above us a fairly dry ten feet led to the top. It was bulging with good holds such as wild rose, broom and birch seedlings. 'Never trust heather,' admonished the Doctor, as we turned to go, 'all right in ropes, but — '

'Hi!' from below. We had forgotten the Apprentice. The Doctor gave me a pebble. I placed it under my boot as support, leaned out from my root and looked down.

The Apprentice was in trouble. My last swim had kicked away every hypnaceous deception. Between us lay a black slab, wrinkling only with water.

The Doctor looked. 'No go in vibrams,' he said. 'Try it in socks. One pair only, mind. Tie your boots round your neck, out of the way. Or to the end of the rope; but they'll get wet there.'

Bitterly, the Apprentice, on his foot-square bath-mat, removed his boots and socks. Foolishly, he slung them round his neck (he always loathed walking down in wet boots). He hauled, unashamedly upon the line. The Doctor, myself, and the root, resisted manfully.

I need not recount the inevitable. The slip on one sodden toe, the twist, the grab on the line with both hands, the clatter of falling boots, the flutter of socks. The appalling and — considering his uncertain position — imprudently blasphemous oaths from the sufferer. We landed him at last. The Doctor, in some ways quite sensitive, moved up to let him on. I inculcated the botanical rudiments necessary for the last few feet.

The Doctor sat on the cliff top, smoking his pipe.

'Pity about the boots,' he said. 'Rather a lot of scree on the way down to them — damned uncomfortable. Could go back the same way, but I don't like taking *two* inexperienced chaps down, and we'd better stick together. It's not hard, but it's not easy. Although I grant you it's not a stiff climb like *Constipation*. Just as well, when you go losing your boots. Bad technique that; hope Aggie didn't see us.'

His soliloquy was interrupted by the Apprentice vividly explaining why, in his judgment, our present route should be termed *Diarrhoea*.

'No, it's *Central Buttress Direct*,' said the Doctor. 'A good classical name. Not in the least subjective. And look at that view. There's Schiehallion — unusual from this side. We'll get you down all right. Piggyback, if necessary. Might even meet with old MacPhedran. He humphs yowes about all day. Remarkably tough. He's docked and castrated three hundred lambs in a morning. He'll take care of you all right. And there — look over there — there's Lancet Edge. Wonderful in the sun.'

3

Flies

'Damn these blasted flies!' roared the Doctor, the hundredth time that day. The Apprentice, beginning a similar though more virile malediction, inhaled too great a horde of *Muscidae* and fell back speechless. For each of us, like an island peak, carried his own cloud. Dodging or ducking could never escape it. Bracken and branches beat in vain. Hands were blistered, arms ached. Chitinous and insistent, it clung. And it buzzed and crawled abominably. At times one of us would creep up to unload his cloud on to a companion; and then try to run free. But the companion, unencumbered – in fact, spurred – by the additional burden, would race to repay him. Heads were thrust under water: but on emergence proved even more attractive.

Walking up and walking down that year were enlivened by such performances, and we grew desperate. Camping was intolerable until darkness brought its relief and its midges – at least a familiar, almost hereditary, malady, benign by comparison. And even then the odd nocturnal fly padded damply across our faces. Driven by the horrors of reverberating sleeping bags and ham-and-fly suppers, we carried a tent – translucent with fly-squash and rustling with old wings – to the top of Ladhar Bheinn; but we left one pole in the Doctor's car, and it rained. Another weekend I gasped in a fly at an unpleasant move above The Chasm, and spat us both into space. Later that day the Doctor also came to grief, claiming he had slipped on a handful of the brutes – 'like ball-bearings on a slab'. At the top, the Apprentice solemnly declared he'd been forced to roll a cloud of them up into a convenient chockstone; it had brought the two of us over the crux before dispersing and flying away. They had in fact become part of the climbing scene. But we never got used to them. We would plot, plot in our downhill cursing. How *could* they be defeated?

Sundew, environmentally preferable, was too slow. We had tried flypaper. We hung three flypapers in the sleeve entrance of the Doctor's Mummery tent, and gloated on the speedy arrest of incomers. But we celebrated unwisely, because that night the Apprentice, wriggling out at the call of nature, forgot about the flypapers. His retreat into the alarmed and pitchblack tent, trailing flypapers and sleeve entrance, needs no elaboration. Fly-sprays were expensive, amused the flies and, according to the Doctor, ours (though not his) were dangerous to health. Nylon net bags did not fulfil their promise. They let feet through and leaked at the neck; and in driving one devil out we allowed seven more in. Ointments and suchlike merely provided the creatures with refreshment and an opportunity to linger.

We sat in despair that evening. Each spoke to the other out of his cloud. One learnt to communicate in this Jove-like fashion, through compressed and fly-denying lips.

'I got most of mine from that dead hind on the bealach,' hissed the Doctor. This provoked unkind comparisons. The Apprentice observed, sideways, that next time he'd bring up some bad meat and lose all his flies on to that.

The Doctor sprang up. His cloud re-adjusted itself nimbly.

'Of course! Of course! What about that new chemical they've made? Better than anything so far known for attracting flies — they used it as bait to clear 'em out of Egyptian hospitals. Has a fearful pong. An improvement on some amine or other from a decomposing mushroom. I know a chemist at the University. I'll get him to try for some. Bound to work!' And he fell back contented into his flies.

That Thursday in Daddy McKay's his eyes were alight.

'Astonishing luck. Chemist chap knew all about it. Had

some in the next lab. Musc-a-something or other. Highly poisonous but a dead cert.' He produced a glass tube containing a small evil-looking brown bottle. 'Next weekend we'll try it . . . '

Next weekend was hot and sticky as usual that summer. We entered a pinewood, roaring and metallescent as Kennedy Field. We stopped. The Doctor went ahead. He selected a long pole from the thinnings. He donned surgical gloves, then extracted his tube from the rucksack, very carefully slid out the bottle, and loosened its stopper. Throttles were opened. He disappeared behind a hurricane of wings, became a pillar of buzz. Then slowly, miraculously, the pillar condensed into a ball and the ball raised itself above him, far above, clustering on the end of the pole. He signalled us to replace the bottle and its tube into his rucksack, then strode on ahead, bearing the cloud of flies aloft. So we progressed, taking turns to hold the pole, bringing its end cautiously near any head visited by less perceptive Diptera. No vacuum cleaner could have done the job better.

Indeed miraculous; if somewhat odd in appearance. We mounted the plateau (it was the Gorms that weekend), and the air cleared. We gingerly laid down the pole and bolted a hundred yards or so. Only a distant revelling. We were safe.

'Marvellous stuff. Pity it's so poisonous. He only let it out because I'm a quack. Seems it's a sure thing for the Third World when the molecule's been tidied up a bit. Should get some here after Devolution.'

Coming down that evening, along the other edge of the corrie, was more difficult. No forest, no poles. We did not risk a long grass stem. Suppose it bent . . . Instead, whenever our individual clouds became too irritating, the Doctor stopped and dabbed a boulder. Then we each went and, holding our noses, laid heads as close to it as possible, and so decanted our flies. Behind us, a powerful telescope would have revealed a succession of curiously-vibrating tumuli.

Peace, peace. Sheer luxury of seeing and hearing again. Of owning one's hair.

Then, just before entering the wood — and its convenience

of poles — disaster struck. The Doctor had been the last to exchange flies with the local granite. In completing this transaction he had knelt — on the bottle . . .

A terrible cry. We looked round. An immense cloud, and out of it the Doctor running as if for life. Without his breeches or his rucksack.

When we had all run half a mile, he stopped.

'Damned good job I had on the old linen ones. Just ripped 'em off, pants and all, and legged it. Stuff hadn't soaked through.'

The rucksack had dropped on to the contaminated garments and, like them, would be unapproachable until wind and weather had done their work. The rucksack contained our few spare clothes, and the Doctor would have to remain breekless. He was fortunate in wearing a long tartan shirt. We made him wash thoroughly in the burn and the Apprentice lent him his belt. Tucked in suitably, the sark now resembled a kilt; on the short side, but adequate. The Doctor chose a comfortable stump, after inspecting it for ants. We munched the Apprentice's emergency rations, moist from his pocket.

'I'll come back for the things tomorrow night. No-one'll nick 'em in that state. We'll just have to go cannily down to the car. Don't want to be picked up like this . . . O damn these flies.'

Our descent became hilarious. Peering through my nimbus I saw the Doctor leaping hairily and bonily ahead, a swashbuckling figure fresh from Killiecrankie or, less improbably, Mons Graupius. We spurred him with Hampden cries. He responded with bursts of *Nicky Tams*.

The path passed Glendrumly Castle. We took that stretch cautiously. Young Glendrumly was a keen ornithologist and possessed a troop of bird-feeding aunts who regularly crumbed the turrets. Also he had an uncle who was a part-time lunatic and occasionally cantered about garbed as the Doctor was now. Every window might have been manned. The Doctor was so intent on watching the Castle that he failed to notice a litter of tourists lying exhausted on his right. They sat up in alarm as he fled. We explained we were from the Castle and hurried on.

Though unsettled by this episode and by the unexpectedly warm driving seat, the Doctor relaxed when his hands were on the wheel.

'We'll go through Balqueenie. Some shops might still be open. Souvenirs and stuff. Might get shorts. Bathing trunks.' He brushed flies from the windscreen, and we drove away.

Balqueenie was crowded. The road before us vanished into heaving tweed. Of course, the Highland Games. Balqueenie, if not artistically the summit of such gatherings, is certainly the social peak. We sniffed. We were snobs. We each had our favourite Meeting, and it was not Balqueenie. The Apprentice had lost his voice for Bill Anderson the week before at the *aficionado*'s gathering at Brig o' Dinnie. The Doctor, when subjecting us to an approximate *piobaireachd* outside his tent, was likely to explain he had just heard that particular interpretation at Lochboisdale or Portree. I myself had come second out of three in a race up the local ben at Strath Warsle — a race, it is true, disorganised at an early stage by the landing amongst the original leaders of a hammer, thrown somewhat inexpertly from elsewhere in the programme. Obviously, we were not Balqueenie men; and we enjoyed the Apprentice's graphic suppositions of the ancestry and habits of the more outrageously decorated members of its ecosystem — a regular *Tartanetum*. The gilt-edge of the crowd, in dreepy kilts and clutching equally unconvincing seven-foot-long polished cromags which kept banging into and interlocking with each other, was being continuously photographed — no doubt as Real Jocks — by the more jovial fraternity in T-shirts and paper streamers. Watching good-humouredly were the whiskied red-faced possessors of the more indigenous genes. Aye, bonnie Balqueenie.

The road cleared. The Main Square. We wound down the window a little. At one end stood a group whose prolonged massacre of the accepted European phonetic values reduced even the Apprentice to silence. They, the really Top People, were accompanied by spectacled gentlemen of eastern appearance, heavily decked in smiles and telescopic lenses. About them stood brow-mopping men whose minds had obviously recently been relieved — the organisers. One of the organisers appeared familiar; he occupied a gratifyingly lived-in kilt. His eye brightened when he saw us. The Club Treasurer, in fact.

'Jamieson!' exclaimed the Doctor. 'That's him. Just the man I had to see. I never sent him those subscriptions — after all I promised.'

We drew into the kerb.

'I must apologise. Won't take a minute. Frightful lapse.'

The Doctor seized the door handle and sprang out of the car. He remained — for a split-second — springing, hairy legs Nijinsky-like, horror on his face. He was of course still clad only in his shirt.

Before he touched ground the Apprentice's splitter-second reflex, so welcome to us on many another crux, had whipped a travelling rug out of the back seat and over his descending frame. The Doctor, no less quick on the uptake, swept it round him in an instant, straightened, and then strode majestically forward across the Forum, attired in a somewhat dusty but nevertheless imposing toga of Ancient MacQuarrie. Before he reached Jamieson's group, which had been struck to unaccustomed silence, he had rustled up an almost believable Inverness cape. His breezy address prevailed and we watched, fascinated, as the eyes of Jamieson's companions slowly rose from the long folds of MacQuarrie to the animated bony countenance. Jamieson himself supported the Doctor manfully, though his bonhomie appeared of the anxious kind. The Doctor had no such inhibitions and seemed in great form, the Gentry rapidly responding with shouts of laughter and high whinnying dipthongs. We trusted that our companion would remember to keep gesticulating with his right hand and not with the left, which was required for his rug.

The driver's window was darkened. Inspector McHaig. He appeared subdued. He leaned heavily. We expected a cheerier greeting. Perhaps he thought the Doctor had gone a little too far. Drink and driving.

'Had a good day, lads?'

'Great. And how were the Games?'

'O fine, fine. Mr Jamieson's very pleased. And Royalty was fair chuffed.'

'You look worried, Inspector. Don't mind the Doctor, he's ... '

'Aye, aye; but I'm afraid we've just had bad news ... There's a body on the hill, lads.'

'Can we ... ?'

'No, no. My chaps have gone up to bring it down.'

We'd thought we'd seen the Pitfoulie Land Rover trumpeting and tusking its way through the throng earlier. 'Pitfoulie there as well?'

McHaig darkened further. 'They've just rammed one of my patrol cars. We've filled the ambulance already.'

'Helicopter?'

'Busy with the traffic. Anyway the poor felly'll not be needing us to hurry, by all accounts.'

He looked meaningly at us. 'It's Captain Rawlings for sure, I'm thinking.'

Captain Rawlings. That gentleman had provided the Pitfoulie Mountain Rescue Team and its exuberant competitors with three weeks' invaluable heather-thrashing in the spring, before being entered up finally as 'Not Found'. We had remained unsurprised at this sad verdict. Captain Rawlings had been, it seemed, an English visitor at the Inverfyvie Arms. He stayed a week. He was popular with staff and guests. He was a willing, and successful, hand at the cards. He stood generous drinks on account. And on the Friday morning he had gone out — 'for a walk on the hill'. He would be back late that night.

He was not back late that night. Nor ever. *Cha till e tuille.* And such a fine gentleman. Of course, very much a novice on the hill. He had town shoes. Very inexperienced — why, he'd even carried his suitcase, it seemed; for that, with his spare clothes, was missing as well. And he'd made a careless mistake about his address, so his next-of-kin — abroad, he had said — could not be traced. Tragic indeed.

'Who told you it was Captain Rawlings?' we demanded.

The Inspector looked a little uncomfortable.

'Miss Threadweaver,' he said.

'Miss — ?'

'She's staying at Glendrumly, helping with the junior bird-watching courses. It's Fledgling Week.'

'Did she *recognise* Captain Rawlings?'

The Inspector looked even more uncomfortable.

'Hout, no, man. Who could recognise him after all this time? And this hot weather. But she saw — A Heap, ye ken. Off the Creag Liath path.'

'But we've just come down the Creag Liath path and we've seen no Heap.'

'Well, she *did*,' said McHaig irritably, 'and she rang us up not ten minutes ago and I've sent men out there. She was all upset. Crying. She'd only bairns with her and darena get closer. "O, it's Captain Rawlings, Inspector," she said, "I know it is." '

'How *could* she know a heap was Captain Rawlings?' we persisted.

McHaig hemmed, and tapped the rim of the window. He gazed at the loquacious group across the Square, from which shrieks of well-dividended laughter could be heard. The Doctor's left hand was still firmly in place.

'There was claes and a rucksack.'

'But Captain Rawlings had a suitcase, not a rucksack.'

'He could have had a rucksack inside the suitcase and put it on when he got to the hill. Ye're better with a rucksack than a suitcase on a hill, are ye not?'

The logic was indisputable.

'Besides . . . ' A pause. 'It was not an ordinary heap of claes. There was an awful-like smell coming from it on the wind, if you understand me. And a great cloud of flies. Terrible lot of flies, she said.' He smacked the Triplex decisively. 'It'll be him right enough. Three months, and weather like this. Poor felly. Anyway, my boys are up there, to bring him down, whoever he is. We've got to do it decently and quickly-like, with the Games on.'

The Apprentice and I looked at each other and swallowed hard. We leant over. We wound down the window to its fullest extent.

We began to explain.

4

Finishing off a Top

It was impossible to see anything. Mist pressed about me, determined to stay. There was no hint of wind. Undressed for late July, I was extremely cold. Droplets explored the tail of my shirt. I stood, cursing, as for the last fifty minutes. It was a small comfort to know that within a two-mile radius of this mist, almost certainly *in* this mist, the Apprentice and — more satisfyingly — the Doctor were likewise standing; and likewise at their own particular spots, and likewise for the last fifty minutes. On this God-forsaken bald-headed hag-ridden heap, three thousand feet up.

Why were we thus enchanted? Could we not sit down? There was nowhere to sit but weeping heather. One could keep drier, or less wet, by remaining upright. Drops gathered and crept down back and knees, but to sit invited cold, prolonged and intimate embrace. Then why not move about? Why not indeed, but for an unaccountable loyalty to the Doctor; a loyalty, I discovered later, shared equally, equally unaccountably, by the Apprentice — whose displeasure in such circumstances is even greater than mine, and whose experience of the Doctor is no less. It only remains to add that at the feet of each of us lay a flag on a long pole.

It was, as I said, late July. It was the weekend after that memorable Sunday the Doctor took us up the 'rock climb' behind his brother-in-law's shepherd's cottage; a fortnight, therefore, after we — or rather the Apprentice — had taken him up his first V.S. Those episodes are recounted elsewhere. Sufficient to record that we — the Apprentice and I — had been sorely-wrought men all that previous week: starting violently at hoot of horn, crossing Princes Street only when repeatedly — at length angrily — beckoned by policemen; peering each morning at a doubtful world through a myriad of entangled and imaginary ropes. So that when, on the next Thursday night in Daddy McKay's, the Doctor asked us out yet again, we both cringed involuntarily and the Apprentice in anguish slopped his Glen Riddance over the table.

'No, never mind,' said the Doctor, flashing out his handkerchief and wiping the Guidebook page rapidly dry, 'I'll get you another — same as before, eh? Fine. Another Glen Riddance, Geordie — ach, make it three more — yes, of course, doubles . . . '

To cut the story short, he won us over. It was to be a Very Relaxing Day. We had all had enough of Difficult Routes (here the Apprentice swelled visibly; I kicked him accurately, beneath the table) and this Sunday — we could leave late Saturday, he would pick us up as usual — this Sunday would merely be to Finish Off a Top.

'Not bloody Munros — ' began the Apprentice.

'No, no, not at all,' said the Doctor.

'A Corbet — or a Donald,' I suggested, maliciously.

'If you think — ' roared the youth, gripping his Glen Riddance tighter this time —

'Certainly not,' said the Doctor placidly, gazing down his beak, 'not Munro-bashing. I did all the Munros in that Section thirty years ago; in one weekend, as it happened. Not Munro-bashing. It's Tops.'

'Tops?!!!'

'Much more skilful, much more interesting. You see quite different country. Some of them are damned difficult to find. Not all properly measured, you know. There's one I'm still not sure of. Here it is in the List, d'you see? (Of course they've missed out the initial aspiration — they always spell these names wrong.) We'll go up there just for a stroll. I'm still quite stiff myself, so you two must be really feeling it; one never gets much exercise up and down those artificial routes of yours. We'll go for a leisurely walk, and I'll nip off and collect that little chap. The weather'll be dead clear all weekend — fine and warm and quite settled, the forecast says. You'll just lie and relax. I'll do all the running about. Tops really test a fellow. Munros! I did most of 'em when I was a student.'

'How . . . many . . . have . . . you . . . done . . .?' muttered the Apprentice, in morbid fascination.

'Two hundred and twenty-eight — or two hundred and twenty-nine if you include Beinn Tarsuinn. But I've hardly bagged a new Munro for years. Been after all the confounded Tops I left out before. And I haven't even done one of those since last Easter Meet.' He closed the Guidebook, put away his spectacles and smiled disarmingly. My round.

We crawled out of the tent into a dawn of lemon and blue. An early start, the Doctor insisted, would miss the Heat of the Day and ensure us time to relax among the summit heather while he rattled off in pursuit of the errant Top. Halfway up sweatily endless slopes, peopled by that detestable species, the 7 a.m. midge, we stopped for a second breakfast of warm ham sandwiches. The view was excellent. Probably even the Apprentice did not miss his rocks.

'I've brought something rather interesting,' mumbled the Doctor through his ham, rummaging in his rucksack — the only one with us, and already stuffed with the Apprentice's shirt and my cagoule. He held up triumphantly a small shining cannon-like object.

'You've probably never seen one' — this to the Apprentice. Then to me: 'Pretty good, eh?'

'Looks like a Dumpy level,' remarked the Apprentice, sourly. The Doctor, somewhat crestfallen, confirmed that it was. However, it had belonged to a Father of the Club . . . After further carabiner-like janglings, he produced a diminutive brass alarm clock.

'Aneroid. Sir Hugh's very own. Patient of mine picked it up at a Kirriemuir roup.'

The Apprentice steadfastly chewed at the view. We awaited a clinometer. But it must have remained inside.

By ten o'clock we had traversed sufficient miles of peat-hag to be rewarded by the cairn, beaming pyramidally from the desert horizon. The Doctor had unerringly smelt it out.

'This is the top,' he announced.

'The one you were after?' enquired the Apprentice hopefully rubbing sweat off his shoulderblades.

'No, of course not. Not the Top, but the top. The Munro. It's the fifth time I've been here,' he added. 'Second in summer.'

He poked a boot reminiscently among burnt stems. Sun gleamed on his polished clinkers. He looked suspiciously innocent. Statistics will out.

He knelt and spread the maps. Two maps because, naturally, the elusive Top could be cornered only at the junction of two sheets. It was not named on the maps. It did not even aspire to a contour ring of its own.

'It's a very doubtful Top,' he explained. 'Phillip and Burn — and Gall Inglis as well — thought it *was* one, but they could never get decent sightings. Today's perfect. Absolutely clear. But you see the ground's so flat about there' — digging a long forefinger into a blank area of map — 'that I can't take sightings on these other two points' — prodding at two bald unpronounceable shoulders — 'unless somebody stands up on each of them with, say, a flag.'

The Apprentice and I began to feel a familiar feeling. We avoided each other's eyes.

'Now if you two chaps would be good enough just to pop over to those two points — see them over there — and stand on them and wave a flag when you see me wave mine: then I can get accurate sightings and we'll soon know the Real Height of this top . . . Phillip and Burn could never do it. Nor Gall Inglis. Make a good Note for the *Journal*.'

'What about . . . a Flag?' I asked, mechanically.

He rooted again in his rucksack. From its lower leathern recesses, Dent-Blanche-battered, he produced a cluster of mahogany brass-ringed rods. He fitted them together.

'From Lamond Howie's tripod. Just the thing. And here's the cloth — bits of the wife's old curtains. Shove the spike through 'em. There's your flag.'

He handed us each our pole and flag, and dismissed us cheerily. We had not the heart to protest.

That had been two hours before. Flag in hand, I reached my imperceptible prominence. Across a deep corrie dozed an identical whale, surmounted by a tiny figure. Another figure, equally remote but recognisable by its bony stride, denoted the Doctor, scaling his debatable contour. His flag danced, a speck of colour, as he climbed. At the top he would wave it. I prepared to stretch out in the sun.

Then out of that blue-eyed sky the mist appeared. Suddenly. Wet, white, annihilating.

Of course, it would lift. It was bound to lift. A mere midday aberration. A casual stray. Rising air would shift it.

It stayed. Fifty minutes, as I said. An hour and a quarter.

Enough. I sighed; I gazed at the pole, I bent down and gripped it. I would go, Doctor or no Doctor. The mahogany and brass gleamed. Sun. Sun . . . .

I looked up. Blue indecision, but blue.

Across the corrie, the whale oozed into view. Upon it a faithful figure. I waved my flag. He lifted his, not with enthusiasm. I guessed his feelings. And the Doctor? Smoke lay thick on Sinai; but it was clearing, clearing. Then — hell and damnation. Clamminess hugged again, and all was lost.

Twice this happened. At intervals of half an hour.

Then it became darker, and drizzled. Low cloud had joined us.

So I bent down, gripped the pole firmly, and strode off.

But where to . . . ? This way, keeping the corrie on the right. But where *was* the corrie? That would be the edge? Peat hag? No . . . Yes? Yes.

I halted, embarrassed. I was about to become lost on this hopeless plateau, *sans* food, *sans* map, *sans* compass, *sans* torch, in shirt and breeks and carrying a mahogany pole with a piece of curtain material on it. And doubtless over there, on his invisible whale, the Apprentice faced the same fate, but without even a shirt . . .

The weather being Settled, this cloud could last for days. I must obviously descend into the corrie. Forty-eight hours' circling on the plateau could never be lived down. Think of the Accident Report. Think of Daddy McKay's. Think of the shrill glee of The Weasels . . .

The corrie revealed itself bleakly and blackly as I went lower. Six miles down the glen, a shooting lodge. Then four miles to a public road. After that, twenty odd more round to the Doctor's car on the other side of the hill . . .

Two peat-haggard hours later I overtook the Apprentice pulling his feet out of a bog. He had passed the savage state, and the weeping state. He was impervious to all, and merely nodded. A dark green stain down his neck indicated where at one time in his vigil he had tried to clothe himself in his flag. (My own was red.)

We reached a puddled track and trudged on silently, in thin sheets of sweeping rain. Wind had arrived, and chased hungrily over vanishing slopes. We half-hoped the Doctor might still be up there, checking his watch. But of course, with map and compass, he would be down at his car. Or perhaps — we must both have thought of this together, for we stopped and looked at each other — perhaps he had back-tracked on bearings to each of our lonely stances, to collect us . . .

No help, we were down. If he was up, looking for us, hard luck.

The Lodge came into view. Large shiny limousine. Early shooters, awaiting August; or landlord inspecting before the let. Probably the latter. A sniffy-looking cove in tweeds emerged from the door, said 'Aah . . . '

Before the Apprentice could reply suitably, I got in with a cordial 'Good afternoon'. Four miles to the public road. You never knew.

'Aah . . . your friend rang up. He'll be round by car presently. Do come in, woncha?'

We stopped, breathed deeply, and turned into the porch-way.

'Aah . . . by the way . . . perhaps you could leave . . . those things . . . out here, eh?

We were still carrying our poles with pieces of curtain on them. We leant them carefully against the ox-blood pine door posts and went inside.

An hour later, a car scritched on the gravel and the Doctor appeared in the room. From our armchairs, we saw him vaguely across the roar of fire, the shine of plates and glasses. The Apprentice, much moved, extended a wavering hairy arm from beneath his thick wool travelling rug.

'Ha,' said the Doctor. 'Knew where you'd skedaddle to when you deserted your posts. Rang up Charlie here — you look fine, Charlie, no more trouble, eh?' (another of his patients, no doubt . . .) — 'rang up Charlie here — yes, thanks, I'll have a Strath Grapple — told him to look after you. Good thing, keeping the flags. Kept mine, too. We'll have another shot next weekend, eh? Settled weather — this is just a local front. Then we'll finish it off, and get back to some real stuff. I'm sure it's a Top all right. The aneroid made it three thousand and two — can I check with your barometer, Charlie?'

5

Chalking It Up

'Come along now, gentlemen, PLEASE,' repeated Daddy McKay almost testily, shepherding glasses on to his impatient tray and flicking his napkin through our animated discussion. But we were slow to leave the back bar that night and the Doctor was still defiant as he struggled into his raincoat at the door, Daddy McKay determinedly freeing a sleeve. 'It's the old days again; the end of your artificial aids.'

He had been lent some Hard Men's Glossies, and his imagination billowed chalk dust and waves of golden Apollos swarming effortlessly up the impossible, ropeless and shirtless (it was the Fawcett era). Climbing was free again, chalk was scarcely an Aid, no more than boots, and quite invisible if tinted to match the rock ('Torridonian would need, let me see, BS 04D43: say, Manders' *Copper Rose* or something like that . . .'). But Scottish orogeny is diverse and contorted, and it seemed a whole palette might be required to satisfy the hues encountered on a single route. The Apprentice, veteran of countless gritted hours with fellow Weasels on rain-battered rugosities, dissolved these calciferous enthusiasms as best he could; he preferred a rope. I, as so often on the hill, followed his lead; for the prospect of trails of polychromatic guano — however tastefully selected — lengthening with the weather down our favourite buttresses, was not attractive. Also, although we appreciated the Doctor's company, and his transport, for frequent escalades of the earlier Scottish classics, we were doubtful of his ability, powdered or plain, to adhere

40

sufficiently to much above Severe (Winter was a different matter). His easy denunciations stung us. So, unwisely, before we parted at the Mound the Apprentice invited him to join us that weekend at the Ben, on a new HVS — just to see what it was like. And equally unwisely, the Doctor agreed.

'Ha, *Constipation*, is it? Yes, I've heard of that. Pretty stiff, by all accounts. But an experience. Even if a limited one: you chaps — .' We choked off another tirade, and pushed him homeward. 'Now mind you mug up your ropework. And no bloody chalk . . . ' was the Apprentice's parting shot. The vision of the Doctor leaping heroically ahead, in dust and bathing trunks, up two hundred leering metres of vertical Lochaber was, that night, most amusing.

It grew less amusing as the weekend approached, and we were strangely silent during the Saturday journey north. The Doctor's old Mercedes lumbered more thoughtfully round the bends in Glencoe, its usual elephantine squeals reined in. After lunch on the shore beyond Ballachulish the Apprentice whistled tunelessly, I plucked grassheads, and the Doctor poked about among seaweed on the boulders. None of us mentioned The Climb, not even by evening when we reached the hut.

We were greeted by the occupants, sundry youths of lurid and basic communicatory skills hailing from the more abrasively north of England. They had, it appeared, gained unlawful entry several days before, and generously offered us the three remaining bunks. Their leader was one Sodder, a formidable XS exponent of whose exploits on alcohol and crag the Apprentice and — since his magazine excursions — the Doctor were well informed. As a large, legitimate and uncompromisingly Glaswegian party was also booked for the hut that night, and was at this instant celebrating thirstily its arrival at the Fort, we gloomily predicted a disturbed prelude to tomorrow's epic.

In the hour or so before the engagement we heard the Englishmen had suffered no trouble from *Constipation* and had, superfluously enough, gone on to take in an adjacent shocking artifical, *Purgative*, dismantling that of aid except halfway up the crux — a quite holdless bulging slab over a horrible, truly aperient, exposure. They had removed even that peg afterwards, for the benefit of their successors . . . It would be at least an XS, climbed free.

The Doctor, scenting chalk, engaged them in earnest conversation. Unfortunately, his incautious extempores in magazine lingo gave them the startled impression that he intended to climb *Constipation* without a rope. The crimson Apprentice was about to cross to the guffaws and explain, when the doorway was filled with Glaswegians; then silence; then expletives.

We managed a few hours' sleep after the battle, one of Bannockburnian intensity and conclusion; and then padded painfully to the foot of our climb. We wore E.B.'s, the Doctor his old gym shoes, bared to the canvas ('probably illegal . . .') and were laden with ironmongery of all configurations and clatter — clusters and panicles of wires, hexcentrics, bongs, étriers . . . and ropes, ropes, ropes. The Apprentice was taking no chances. He kept instructing the Doctor on the red rope, the green rope, the fixed rope, the free rope, this rope and that rope. The Doctor nodded sagely, obviously and irritatingly wishing to understand little of it. As he strode, his coils opened and shut, disclosing a small canvas bag tied to his waistband. Chalk . . . ? Chalk, it must be. If the English saw us . . . From the disgruntled tents of the vanquished far up the Allt a'Mhùillin (whence they could, at their own convenience, pollute the hut's alleged water supply) we imagined the first faint jeers. But we said nothing.

The initial pitches were fairly uneventful: steep dry rock in early sun. The Apprentice had struck form. I followed adequately despite my burden of prophylaxis, and the Doctor rattled up behind, multijointedly competent as a harvestman crossing a flysheet. But he was troubled by the prolixity of ropes. I gathered them up before him, as one conjures the cords of a disobedient Venetian blind. He arrived and cast further superfluity at my feet. 'Most tiresome, all these unnecessary ropes. No wonder they hardly use them nowadays.' He held out his arms like one accepting wool;

I wound him about suitably and turned upwards again.

There were of course minor anxieties. As when the Doctor suddenly stuck. In midswarm. He was surmounting a roof, a narrowing crack on his left. He strained and swore. No use.

'I think I'm stuck.' Then, more specifically, 'These damned things are caught somewhere below.' Further information revealed that he could not spare a single limb, and his neck (surprisingly) was not long enough to allow his teeth full play. Praying and cursing, I secured his ropes and abseiled down. The nuts on the wire slings attached to his harness had travelled beside him up the crack; when it narrowed they had fulfilled the intentions of their designer. Extrication proved lengthy. I relieved him of slings. A similar incident occurred shortly afterwards on an outward-pressing wall, to the anguish of our leader, spread on a balance stance out of sight above; it involved a mysterious loop of rope about the Doctor's rucksack and a mutual tying and re-tying in a parabiotic embrace on a halfhearted wrinkle of rock; it was complicated by a hook in his fishing hat refusing to leave my ear. Clearly he was not to be trusted with this mileage of rope. We were already garlanded grotesquely; soon he would be a cocoon. I pruned him of rucksack, ironmongery and spare coils and left him with a suitably modest bell-pulling repertoire, the bare minimum of attachment.

It is the next pitch, the pendulum pitch, that still shakes our memories. *Constipation* entails only a brief pendulum — as its name implies, it concentrates on a fairly rigid line — but the Doctor, drunk from his liberation, leapt lankily rightward from so far left he outshot the route, collided with a brutal rib on the other side, twisted, and vanished out of sight behind it. He did not come back. I pulled the red rope. No reply. The green one. It pulled back. His seventy-four inches were presumably still consecutive.

Their retrieval was less obvious. The rib cut off sight and coherent sound. Only a muffle. I roared instructions. Only a muffle. Then, a high whoop of derision. It was the English. Even farther to our right, in several parties, on fearsome lines. And much enjoying our plight. The ribaldries of

Sodder were particularly displeasing to the Apprentice, who was informed from that embarrassing source of the fate of our colleague.

'Yer know were e is? E's on *Purgative*. An e's there for keeps. Right under the bloody crux!'

We froze. His return demanded a computery of rope-twiddling impossible to convey through twenty metres of indifferent andesite. And clearly the English were going to enjoy the situation as long as possible. Last night would not soon be forgotten. They began to sing. '*Will yer no come baaack again . . .* '

Pushing rightward on vanishing balance holds the Apprentice managed to look over an impassable gulf to our companion. He shouted down instructions to both of us. No easy task, with the Auld Enemy jamming the wavelength. ('*Boney Chaarlie's noo awaah . . .* '). The inevitable had to happen. The Doctor, none too clear anyway about which of the unidentifiable ropes to clip or unclip or haul or let out, and counterinstructed by the echoes booming about his vertical danknesses, let slip the only line that could have ensured his return to us — that even joined us . . . The end snaked down into limbo. We heard a muffled 'Blast!'

The English, if they were sympathetic, did not show it. The singing stopped.

'E's chucked off is bloody rope like e said e would. E's goin to do *Purgative* solo! Ah, yer can't old im back, can yer? Good ole Golden Boy!' Unfeeling roars of laughter. Whistles, hoots; then '*Scotland the Brave*', much off-key.

Although we knew the Doctor's remarkable powers of survival, we began to sweat. I struggled up slabs and roofs to the Apprentice, and crabbed out to the edge overlooking *Purgative*. The Doctor occupied its one gesture at a ledge, but seemed in good form, hat rammed firmly on, the usual sign of determination. We could not cross down to him; but would have to descend *Constipation*, peg up *Purgative*, work out runners and then somehow gather him in. A long job. He could not abseil from his present position; to climb down was unthinkable; to climb up would bring him almost alongside us, but was equally unthinkable — the crux of *Purgative* free and without protection! And now a thin mist moistened the rocks . . . It might have to be helicopters, or Pitfoulie. O, the shame of it . . . Comment and songs continued ('Come on Jock, straight up, that's it.' 'Yer alfway there already mate.' '*You take the igh road and I'll . . .*').

The Apprentice whipped his ropes and hammered in the first abseil peg. I gazed fascinated at the Doctor.

'Lord, what's he doing now?' The Apprentice paused; and stared, too. The singing stopped. Whistles died.

He had hauled his loose end back, tied it in a loop and, after a couple of shots, miraculously lassoed an evil razor-edged spike to his right. A parapsychological belay, indeed. He looked up, saw us, grinned, and waved perilously. And then, balancing outward against all his years of Alpine anecdote, put his hand surreptitiously into his little canvas bag.

'Chalk! He's not going to try the crux on CHALK?!!!'

His hand emerged, pressed the rock in front of him firmly, patted it, and returned to the bag. Then he patted the rock a little higher up, similarly.

Chalk? The English were as dead silent as us. Sodder was poised on one toe and a finger, agape. Chalk?

A few more gropings in the bag and pattings, and he began to move up the appalling bare bulge of slab that gave *Purgative* its name. Not true. Our mouths cracked with drought.

He groped again. More pattings. And up another metre or so. The crux is not so vertical as impossibly smooth and holdless. Yet he climbed the six metres of it as deliberately as if he were moving from invisible pimple to pimple, or pick-scratch to pick-scratch as in his tales of the moonlit Brenva; even the venomously gentle detachment of belay from spike did not disturb him. One slip . . .

Incredibly, falling was far from our thoughts. We were hypnotised by his proceeding up that unthinkable slab. Of course, he had a Glenmorangie reach, but . . .

He was suddenly just below us on the right. He had climbed the crux. He gripped, white-knuckled and thankfully enough, its final rim. He grinned. A deep breath, and he mantelshelfed on to a stance, stood up, stretched, and rubbed his arms.

'Can you chuck me a rope? Might as well use one now. The rest's a doddle, but the easy bits are always the most dangerous . . . And all your tomfoolery took it out of me at the beginning.'

Our emotion was great as we lassoed his outstretched arm, and became greater with the applause from across the cliff, punctuated by only a few face-saving catcalls. The English are sportsmen yet.

The respectful spell was somewhat broken by a subsequent barrage of queries. They possessed the same tenor:

'Ow the — — did a daft ole — like that get up *Purgative*?'

How indeed? When we finally all arrived at the top of *Constipation*, which gave us little trouble after our remedial dose of its neighbour, the Apprentice and I, still trembling, put the question in less generally philosophical terms.

'What the devil have you got in that bag? Plaster of Paris?'

He smiled avuncularly, and untied the canvas. He held it high and shook it upside down over the Apprentice's doubtful palm. Two or three moist conical objects dropped out.

The Apprentice drew his hand away hurriedly. The objects fell to the scree. The Doctor bent and picked them up.

'Lucky I had enough. I was just running out.'

'What *are* they, for heaven's sake?' We stared uncomprehendingly. The answer was simple. He held it out.

'Limpets. *Patella vulgata*. Got them yesterday on the shore. Not the rockpool sort, but the real knobbly high-water-mark jobs. Tough; used to exposure. Can stand waves of 25 tons to the square yard. Thought they might come in handy. Winthrop Young recommended 'em. Of course you put your weight on 'em gradually. Give 'em time to suck. Too quick dislodges 'em. Interesting technique.

'Not really artificial: sort of Combined Tactics — after all, they *are* alive . . . '

We were still speechless.

'Ha, you thought they were chalk? So they are — chalk on the hoof. It's lucky the rock got damp just then and kept 'em happy; though I did bring some sea water, just in case.'

We rattled down the path. Neither the Apprentice nor I, still shaking, could face Tower Ridge, and the Doctor was not keen to descend *Purgative*. 'You know, they're chancy beasts.'

That evening Sodder came down, to see the Doctor. They had a long discussion, as between equals. Sodder went away after only half a bottle of Strath Hashie; he appeared pre-occupied.

'He's going to try *Purgative* solo tomorrow.' We asked about the limpets. 'I mentioned them in passing. I don't think he took it in. You technicians are terribly limited. And it'll rain tonight. He'll never see them. They'll have moved, or been eaten, by the morning. You know, you need a fresh lot each time.'

6

Once in a While

Skiing is a vice few of us can altogether avoid. I had succumbed to temptation several times, once even tasted a polythene-wrapped package course under sardonic Continental instruction. The Apprentice, well trained by early glissades in vibrams down Twisting Gully, took to it readily. Goggle-hats and numbers fitted in well when he felt too tired for climbing or when the particular bird-in-hand leaned agreeably towards *après-ski* complaisance. Obviously our ski-tracks did not often cross. Moreover, the Doctor's performance on boards, though darkly hinted at, remained unknown to us.

One weekend, however, we did, more or less, ski together. The Apprentice's girl friend and his mini-van had both suffered mechanical failure at the last moment. Snow was flour on marble, good for ski-ing, shocking for gullies. He came to my door on the Saturday morning, disconsolately magnificent in heliographic steel-and-plastic boots, and carrying the glittering balance of a hundred pounds sterling on his shoulder. Such splendour in distress moved me to pity, though I preferred the kind of sartorial ostentation more usually displayed by The Weasels — rusted ironware and egg-hardened rags. Could I, would I, join him? But I had no car that weekend either . . . We thought of the Doctor, our traditional transport in emergency. We rang him up.

'Where were you off to? Glen Scree? Ha, so was I. Excellent snow I believe. Jolly good idea. Like to see how you fellows ski. You can't have been at it very long . . . ' So he met us with his old Mercedes and we strapped our planks aloft, beside a long leather canoe-like object.

At Glen Scree the fair was in full swing. We took down our skis. The Doctor unlaced the canoe and drew out a pair of huge sledge-runners, turned up fully a foot at each solid hickory toe. He laid them massively down, then extracted two long bamboo poles, ending in plate-sized wattle baskets. A large shapeless rucksack appeared on his back. As he wore his regular poacher-pocketed climbing tweeds, fishing hat, gaiters and clinkered boots he struck uncommon silence into the chromatic throng about us. Shouldering his burden and scattering lesser fry, he strode off. We had agreed to go on to the plateau, although the Apprentice, dreaming of effortless thousands of feet of Jaguar (a curiously revolting Grade II descent), remained reluctant. I followed. The Apprentice roared at us over the juke-boxes.

'You're not *climbing* up? What's the lift for?'

The Doctor smiled benignly across an open sea of mouths.

'We can't waste time on a lift. We're late already. I told you, you should have brought your skins.' He turned, causing a travelling ripple of ducking, and marched on. I hurried after him.

When the crowd had thinned sufficiently for us to see the snow beneath us, we stopped and put on skins. The Doctor produced from his rucksack two seven-foot lengths of genuine seal skin. 'Damned fine animal it must have been,' he said reverently as he buckled the harness. 'Never let me down in twenty-five years. Tore out a big chunk on a tin the first time we did the Haute Route, and lemmings ate a bit that Lapland trip; but there's always enough left for patching.' He pulled the last thong tight and stepped aboard into great hinged and bolt-headed bindings. A pause to press his pipe; then he clanked away elk-like and I shuffled after, in unyielding contemporary footgear. No wonder the Apprentice — who would be clamped irreversibly flat to aluminium and fibreglass — preferred the chairlift.

Hoots followed us from the queue where that metallescent youth was indulging in ignoble gibes.

'Can't think how he can waste good ski-ing time — never mind money — on those antiquated sack-elevators,' remarked the Doctor, plunging upwards through a Gate. A local Beer Trophy was being run, and I scuttled alongside, ears burning.

True enough, we were quite a way up before the Apprentice reached the end of the queue. Then he whisked above us, attempting to spear the Doctor's hat with a flash of Japanese chrome steel. 'I'll get a couple of runs in while I'm waiting for you,' he shouted. Waggling his glitter in triumph, he vanished into the blue. I heaved along grimly, exiguous on icy rubble. The Doctor, well ahead, elaborated on the superior rhythm of climbing in skins. 'Now even with trikes your feet would be slipping about in a place like this. Effortless with skins.' Push. Slide. Push. Slither. Slide. Push.

We climbed higher. We stopped once to reassemble a gentleman in an ankle-length cagoule and a label. My companion felt him all over, pronounced him fit as a fiddle, slapped him on the back and returned him to his erratic and billowing descent. He did not get far. 'Carrying too much sail,' observed the Doctor. Push. Slide. Push.

Nearly there. Above us an individual appeared at great speed, bent in a stiff right-angle. We paused. Ski-sticks and expression fixed unwaveringly ahead, legs wide apart, he charged past us to the enemy below. Appropriately, he was capped with a Balaclava. Our respectful resumption was momentarily interrupted by the trajectory of his Instructor, bewailing the errant lamb — 'Benzeneez, benzeneez' — and cursing fluently in Austro-Glaswegian. The rest of the flock clutched each other on the pebble-dash wall above. We agreed the slopes were busy enough for the time of year. Slither. Push. Slide. Push.

The air rarefied and I became aware of a great silence. We had topped the corrie. The upper station of the lift lay just visible on our left. No sign of the Apprentice. 'He's probably gone down again for his run,' I remarked, not without envy.

'We can't wait all day. If he doesn't come by the time I've finished waxing, he's obviously funked it,' said the Doctor. 'Seems to admit he needs more practice. Though I'm not at all sure we haven't beaten him. Those things are so slow.'

We had in fact beaten him, as we discovered later. At that moment, and for the next three hours, the Apprentice, blue as his boots, was dangling thirty feet above icy scree in a cold iron chair, consoled by a boisterous north wind. The drive sprocket or some such appendage had jammed. The papers made a lot of it the next day.

Meanwhile, the Doctor applied a glistening tar-like concoction, smelling of Andalsnes boat-yards, to his considerable square-footage. He rubbed each hull energetically with a slab of cork, explaining the eminent practicability of this composition. 'Your plastic soles'll be ripped to pieces on any really interesting bit of ground. All *I* need do is give another rub — just like this — and be as smooth as ever. Sure you don't want some?' I declined, but my apprehensions, always alert in the Doctor's company, shifted uneasily.

No Apprentice. 'The lad's not coming. Playing at Sliders. Even a lift can't take as long as this. Let's go.' And the Doctor poled off bonily across diamonded whiteness.

There was an uncanny lack of orange peel. There were no other tracks. The sun shone out of a cloudless sky. Miles of glistering plateau. The Doctor was moved to song, not one of his several accomplishments. I cruised behind, lulled by the more agreeable purr of powder beneath smooth plastic. Bliss.

Yes, it was a good day, although, being early January, a short one. I steered him away from the worst stretches of dragon's teeth ('nothing like rough stuff to test your technique!'). I followed gratefully his tracks, twin country lanes, through fathoms of drift. I skidded, marvelling, above his flagship manoeuvrings on steep ice (gold would not have tempted me beneath them — nor within range of his poles, wielded with true Bannockburn fervour). I drank unashamedly his ice-cold wine and tea at our farthest point. 'Nothing like it; cools you and warms you at the same time. Just the thing for today. I bet *he's* slogging beer right now, hogging the fleshpots between runs. Must have done tens of thousands of feet — but he's young, and needs the practice. Takes a long time to learn how to ski.'

We sailed leisurely back. At times, I clattered frantically
and expensively across windsawn patches of granite and
heather; the Doctor did not appear to notice them, being
occupied with his pipe, which was not drawing well that day
('this damned north wind'). At times, too, I narrowly escaped
engulfment by the craters his baskets left among the polished
windslab.

His falls, for — mercifully — he too had falls, were collapses
worthy of such imperial progress. When the powder clouds
had blown away, crossed limbs and hickory stood magnificent
in ruin against the landscape. A grunt, then Ozymandias himself creaked and elevated out of the depths, raising himself
with impossible flexions of hinge, leather and tendon. He
would dust himself down, search for his pipe, and explain at
length how, given that precise conjunction of dynamics and
metereology, such a fall in such a direction in such snow was
quite inevitable; almost, it seemed, praiseworthy. After
which, climbing over the rim of his late demonstration, he
would punt away, apparently satisfied. He was, however,
notably more cautious for fully three minutes after each fall,
and later in the day I detected a slight limp and a recurrent
reindeer-like clang as if some weight-bearing machinery had
come adrift in his bindings; but there seemed more than
enough to spare and our speed remained respectably high on
the Amundsen scale.

At last we returned to our starting point, not far from the
top station. The Doctor cast anchor with both sticks, fiddled
a chain or two and sprang lightly ashore. Puffing his pipe, he
raised seven feet of hickory and examined below waterline,
to the wonder of a small crash-hatted green-goggled urchin,
Number 10.

'Hm, not bad. Picked up very few stones this time. Excellent w x. Pity I've almost finished the last barrel. Comes in
drums now; not half so good.' Then he suddenly straightened
up and dropped his timber, pinning beneath it the fluorescent
ski-lets of Number 10. 'There he is! Just coming off the lift.
For the nth time, I'd say. Look how he's staggering. Punch-
drunk, these fellows.' The Apprentice indeed slid drunkenly

towards us, skis crossed, eyes staring. He had in fact just been released from his three-hour dangle at minus five. He could not speak.

The Doctor picked up his skis, reassuringly patted the liberated Number 10, and climbed back into the cockpit. He put away his pipe and prodded the still speechless Apprentice with a monstrous basket (I was fascinated by the curved iron hook beneath it). He beamed invitingly.

'Come on, now — a race down, eh? Give us ten yards' start; remember you've been practicing all day, and we're stiff.'

He sculled furiously off, leaving black streaks on the snow.

A couple of wee smashers, preening nearby, tittered.

My leader of a hundred icy cruxes, the Apprentice is nothing if not game. He rumbled some improbable liquid-nitrogen oath, rolled eyes to the sky, and hurled himself stiffly down. I followed, circumspectly. It was, after all, Jaguar.

There is a small rock island near the middle of Jaguar. The Doctor, leaning back contemplatively in a shower of ice, rode his sticks like an experienced cavalry general; a tug at the reins, and he was carried off safely leftwards, out of the fray. The Apprentice, bombing down inert and frozen, remembered too late. Jaguar struck — hard. He somersaulted several yards and continued, mercifully beyond teeth and claws, on his back, head foremost. Eventually he came to rest, against a pair of spectators. The Doctor, completing his hundred-metre flourish, sallied in on one knee, bent in a pensive Telemark. He slowed gracefully to a halt; rose, and leaned, sticks beneath chin. He looked down, Wellington from his horse. The spectators held gloved hands in silence.

'Well, well. You fellows just do too much Downhill for one day. You should take time off, sit around a bit. Chair and a nice cold beer in the sun for an hour or two. That's what I'd do if I had to stay and practice here. Not race up and down like this. You get careless. Lose control. Must keep control on a mountain, you know; otherwise, even ski-ing can become dangerous.' He and the sun gleamed together, through gold-rimmed Polaroids.

The Apprentice glared up weakly. His crash hat was dented. Small blue fragments lay about him on the snow.

In the bar we grew mellow. The Apprentice was gratefully welcoming back his various joints. 'Oh, ski-ing's good fun once in a while,' said the Doctor, raising his Glen Rauchle, 'but not a patch on glissading. Glissading's straightforward. Don't need all these contraptions. But mind you, one thing you do need' — he tipped back reminiscently — 'you do need a good long axe.'

7

Sportsmanship

'The sport of mountaineering ought not to be conducted so as to interfere with the sport of shooting.' The Doctor finished his quotation from the Club Guide, closed the book with a righteous snap and stuffed it back in his rucksack.

'Well then, what do we do?' asked the Apprentice irritably.

Of course, we shouldn't have been there on a late September Thursday afternoon, bang (we crouched apprehensively) in the middle of Inversightie deer forest. But coincidence of a sudden holiday, glorious sun, and a fine new route on the Upper Corrie, had overcome scruples. We had done the climb, lazed the tops and were lolloping down long heathery slopes. Then we had seen glittering beads — Range Rover, Land Rover and some hermaphroditic kind of Terrain Vehicle — parked below in the glen. We had sunk in the heather. We felt horribly exposed.

Indeed, a dilemma. To crawl away unseen would risk intercepting an accidental high-velocity rifle bullet. To rise and march brazenly down would, though satisfying the Apprentice's political views, upset the sport and possibly risk intercepting a not so accidental high-velocity rifle bullet. One never knew. Stalking was Big Money these days, and Inversightie was now in the hands of a London leisure syndicate. Their guests could include any aggressive entrepreneur.

The Doctor scanned the hill with his Trinovids. He searched for stalkers, not stalked. He found both, and worked out a route. If we were quick, we could slip between hairy hide and

Harris tweed; unseen, unheard and unsmelt. The ground was peat-haggy enough to protect us from all except mortar fire.

He led away, wriggling from sopping depression to depression. We followed, groaning silently, elbows and knees soaked. The Doctor's tweeds were better than terylene for this vermicular progress; the hairs acted as *setae*; and wetness remained warm, mud invisible. Every so often he raised a tweed-clad head. We were still safe; on one side, ten points grazing; on the other, six backsides crawling; all seven intent on the day's business, not on us. Our sympathies lay with the stag, not with the plump executive doups. Through the glasses we saw the beast browse; sniff, lower, and browse again. It moved from patch to patch, a ripple of sunlit muscle. It would soon be sausages. We consoled ourselves by making merry at the guests' expense, which must already have been considerable.

We were just about to leave a large green saucer of watercress, and the Doctor had breasted the top of its heathery rim, when we heard a burst of hissing, like a conflagration of snakes. Astonishment radiated down on us, together with a metallic clatter; and then loud furious whispers.

'Damnation, who the devil are *you*, sir?' breathed an unknown but tightly-buttoned court-martial voice.

'Confound it, I could ask the same of *you*, sir!' we heard the Doctor stoutly breathe back. We sank deeper into dank stalks, the Apprentice purple with suppressed mirth.

The Doctor and the stranger had met eye-to-eye at the top, each having crawled up, with elaborate precautions, from opposite sides. Chagrin was mutual. The stranger received such a fright he had let go his rifle; hence the clatter. With dreadful consequences.

'Damnation, damnation, you have lost me my beast!' The stag was no longer grazing. It had vanished. This was serious. But our leader was up to it.

'Confound it, man, you have lost me *mine* — dropping your rifle; dash it, *dropping your rifle*! The whole corrie echoed!' The Doctor pointed to the hillside behind the stranger. 'Look — nothing there now!' Which was true.

The stranger was clearly unsettled. He paused. He cleared his throat. He asked the Doctor over; he produced a flask, apologies, and his name. Colonel Gow-Gow. Embassies were established. As the Doctor crawled over, he divested himself of rucksack and signalled us to stay put. We glanced behind us. The other hunters continued, obviously after a different stag.

Colonel Gow-Gow was, despite his name, alone. 'My man is away down the corrie. With the other two of the party.' Sad days for Inversightie: one stalker to three gentlemen — if they were gentlemen; the Colonel's intonation suggested the others were not. We heard the Doctor intimate that *his* man (and presumably his rifle) were behind, together with a gillie. Colonel Gow-Gow paused again, disconcerted by this suggestion of a retinue. He went on, more rapidly, 'I think *my* man said some *climbers* were coming down the glen. He's gone to give 'em hell. The most stupid, selfish, devils, climbers. Always going out and getting lost and killing other people *looking* for them. I'd leave 'em to rot.' 'I'm sure,' agreed the Doctor. 'Selfish swine, spoiling a whole day's sport — *one man* —' hissed the Colonel (his voice was crimson) 'one man can spoil a *whole day's* sport for people who've had to travel hundreds of miles to get it.' 'And some have had to pay hundreds of pounds to get it, as well,' added the Doctor, genially. The Colonel stopped, and cleared his throat; he nosed to a different line. 'Changed days at the old place now. Not like when the Duke was here. *Then* we had some good times!'

Having inferred his at least previous eminence, the Colonel was moved to pour out another dram; we heard the glob-glob. Then smacking of two pairs of lips. Below stairs, we thirsted. (One pair smacked like boots on a doormat; we guessed (correctly) that the Colonel had protruding teeth and a moustache.) 'Went off jolly sudden, didn't he, the old Duke?' said the Doctor, still lip-tasting. 'Got a shock when I read about it,' agreed the Colonel. 'Happened to be at the house with him that day,' remarked the Doctor casually, 'he never recovered consciousness after dinner.' (The Doctor had indeed been at the ducal residence that day, called over from the campsite hastily in a professional capacity.) The point was taken, and Gow-Gow was noticeably more respectful. 'Errrhghm; might as well finish this dashed stuff, eh?' Glob-glob. Smack-smack. Sighs.

'Well, I'll just carry on over the hill,' said the Doctor, kindly. 'I feel we haven't lost him yet.' 'I hope you haven't, sir, I *hope* you haven't,' devoutly wished the Colonel, 'shall I see you back at the — ah — house?' (he could not say 'hotel'). 'Probably not, probably not,' replied the Doctor, gazing past Cairn Toul, 'I can't *bear* to see what's going on there now. I have — more or less — ah — my own — ah — special arrange-ments — not, you see, ah — in a Party . . .' He smiled equally distantly and slithered away, beckoning us to follow well to the right. Our procession left a deflated Colonel, stagless and whiskyless. Also, mud was up his barrel.

Much amused, we wormed on. Some twenty minutes later, we elbowed on to a track; we judged it safe to get up and walk.   Immediately, a ferocious blast of hot air hit us.

'What the hell are you doing here?'   Most discourteous. The stalker. A tall man, black as the landscape, with pinebark complexion and expression like a granite cliff; and with curiously shifting black eyes.

The Doctor carefully took him in.

'Andrew, Andrew, that's a fine way to greet us.'

Instantaneous effect. Huge hands clasped his. 'Man, man, it's yourself, so it is. Ah, Doctor, Doctor.'

This pleasing emotion, we learned, was due to the Doctor's having saved Andrew's life when a guest had shot him instead of a stag (another call from the campsite). The Doctor had thus performed the most valuable service in the world. Andrew, it seemed, would do anything for him.

'Now, can I help you at all, Doctor?'

This time we all sampled the flask. (Climbing was not men-tioned.) We spoke of the Colonel, and how he had dropped his gun and lost his beast. Andrew had indeed been the Colonel's 'man'.

'What, yon havering old goat? Comes here for a day and orders you about as if he were — as if he were on a Fortnight's

Executive Special, Royal Introductions and all . . . I left him to it.' Andrew spat. He was an emotional man; and maybe remembered other days. We asked about the rest of the Colonel's party.

'Just come up from them. Left them on the road. I'm taking the Range Rover down to pick 'em up. Now, let me give you a lift . . . och, there's room.' We enquired gently about the fate of the Colonel. 'Oh, damn the Colonel. I'll send a boy up for him later. His ticket runs out at six o'clock anyway: that's another full day he'll have to fork out for. Mean old sod. Never a tip. Aye on about his pension. I'd pension him.' We asked again about the remaining guests.

'One's a Dutchman; drunk. And the other's a Jap,' said Andrew, stretching his head out of the window and pulling the wheel round hard. 'Both industrialists. Both too fat. Both good sports. Just here for the hell of it.' We jolted over the ruts. Then: 'Now, here's something you can perhaps do for *me*, Doctor' — Andrew changed into second and glanced sidewise at our companion.

The Japanese gentleman was to fly home that night. He had been a week at Inversightie, his only glimpse of the British Isles, and still had not seen — a Duke. It was once the home of a Duke, the brochure had said. He would so like to see a Duke. Could Andrew not find him a Duke to see? (Here our driver looked meaningly at us all, leant back and patted his trouser pocket; he was clearly a practical man.) Now — he changed into third as the surface improved — what about the Doctor being a Duke? The Doctor would look the very part — tall, distinguished — here Andrew laid it on unhesitatingly, with sidelong shifts of his bright black eyes (to produce which his father, a dour Speysider, had eventually to marry Maureen Mary Maguire, on the old Duke's former Killarney estate).

The Doctor was entertained. 'Right, I'll be a Duke for the next few miles.' But when we reached the venue, there was no Japanese. Only the Dutchman, flat as a polder. He had been sick. Andrew jumped out and roused him ungently. He was pushed in, rubbing eyes. Apparently the Japanese had been given a lift by someone else back to the hotel; the Nederlander was too well sluiced, half Zuider Zees over, to be admitted to a car. He began, in fact, to embrace Andrew and was heaved behind the back seats, where he resumed his snores. Tight as a windmill, and in no state to be impressed by nobility. Andrew and the duke-elect therefore discussed the Japanese, who had insisted on going out to stalk in the kilt he had bought in Balqueenie. 'But the midges?' No bother; he had kept on his long cotton underpants. Andrew shook his head in admiration.

'There he is!' Outside the hotel gates, taking photographs of his late crew. When he saw us, he trundled over, lenses flashing, long-johns winking through the tartan.

'Mr Matsui, I have a great surprise for you.' 'For me, for me? Thank you, thank you.' 'I have the honour to introduce to you a gentleman who expressed a great desire to meet the President of the, of the . . . ' 'Koriyanagishigamatsu Corporation,' gleamed Mr Matsui, arm outstretched, ' . . . of the Corporororation,' continued Andrew ('he *is* drunk,' the Apprentice whispered, 'he *must* be') ' . . . His Grace, His Grace the Duke, THE DUKE OF GLENLIVET . . .'

The Doctor lightly extended three fingers, eyes aglint . . . Mr Matsui seized them and bowed deeply, kilt (Ancient Matheson) sweeping the ground. The Duke nearly overbalanced, but managed to get free in time. He inclined his head, graciously.

'Excuse, my Duke; a photograph.'

Click.

And another lens.

Click.

Two steps back, and a huge lens.

'One moment, my Duke.' A tripod appeared and extended itself. M. Matsui pressed something, skipped and joined us, smiling up at the Duke.

Delayed action.

Click.

We all relaxed. Smiles were passed round, several circuits. The Duke, reluctantly, could not accept the so kind invitation to the hotel. He had to be back. To see, presumably, to his dukedom. More handshaking, bows, inclinations, scuttling of smiles. We left, Andrew accompanying Mr Matsui with a straight face, grim as Braeriach; invisible clouds of blarney played about him.

'A pleasing rogue in some ways, Andrew,' was the ex-duke's comment as we trudged to Balqueenie. 'Tells me he'll be head stalker soon. Never got beyond pony-man in the old boy's time; but he probably suits the new owners — or they him.'

We had a good meal in Balqueenie and were walking towards the Doctor's car when a taxi passed us. It stopped. It was Mr Matsui, returning to Japan, via Dyce. He and the Doctor, a Duke once again, chatted. The Doct . . . Duke . . . had of course visited Japan; and climbed mountains. And toured shrines. And seen castles. They were soon deep in the Katsura Imperial Villa at Kyoto. 'Such a difference the lay-out there to the warrior garden of the Shogun's — *that* was all bristles,' smiled the Duke, 'like Colonel Gow-Gow.'

'Ah, you know Go-Go! I tell him I meet a Duke. Long thin gentleman in knee-breeches. Who had been on hill. He very upset. He meet you before and he not know — you were Duke!' 'Ah, there's no point in blazoning it about nowadays,' shrugged our nobleman. Mr Matsui gazed up admiringly.

Just then a ragged unwashed crowd appeared, dangling helmets and karabiners, singing a loud improper song. Some of the Weasels. They hooted at their fellow-member, the Apprentice. They knew the Doctor, and came over to us. They slapped him on the back unceremoniously — 'Hi Doc, been sunning yer erse all day, eh?' and suchlike remarks well out of protocol. The Duke bore it, but eased himself and Mr Matsui away. The latter had clasped his hands together. (We trusted he had taken 'Doc' for 'Duke', and had inferred some linguistic relaxation.)

'So wonderful. Democracy. Now I *do* understand your country: all in same boat, now. Beautiful!' Then, briskly, 'One more picture, please.' He snapped the Duke, who looked less happy, among the riotous Weasels. One of them was bowing. Another held his nose. Had that swine of an Apprentice hinted anything?

Mr Matsui popped back into the taxi. He shook hands through the window with the Duke repeatedly, as it gathered speed. The Duke trotted alongside, clutched inextricably.

'So wonderful to meet you, dear sir, so wonderful. Such experience to meet gentleman who so — ' here he let go, mercifully, and continued leaning out of the window, waving ' — so like *real* Duke in storybook . . . '

The Doctor rejoined us, exhausted. We never decided what Mr Matsui meant. His English was poor. But he was a very successful industrialist. The Doctor did not ask Andrew; those West Kerry eyes . . . Perhaps a joke had been worth more yen than a mere introduction.

As we lay back in the car, we saw the Colonel. He paused, then hurried across. The Doctor skilfully slipped into gear, and waved briefly. The Colonel's smile died, his carefully prepared apology remained undelivered. He diminished in the rear window, tail wagging slower and slower, bone dropped.

His ex-Grace slowed, sighed, and mopped his brow. He pushed his coronet into the gloveshelf. He did not join our conversation. It had been a tiring day. Some miles later, he delivered his conclusion.

It was that, all being equal, the sport of mountaineering ought to be conducted so as not to be interefered with by the sport of shooting.

8

The Loosening Up

The doctor was leading. At least, he was in front. The Apprentice was below me. We all waited. We were all, so far, on a dirty face beneath Càrn Righ. The time was a grey east-windy November afternoon and far too late. This excursion had begun as a loosening-up for the winter and the Doctor, loose enough, had suggested a final scramble up the sputter of crags before we snuffed the day out with Càrn Righ. 'I brought a rope anyway, in case,' he said.

So here we were. Càrn Righ, tired of waiting, had turned back into mist. But the weather was becoming interested in us. Gusts sniffed, and I swore I saw snow. That east wind . . .

'What the hell's the matter?' I shouted again. The rope, ridiculous twins of baby nylon, twirled up round an assemblage of idle blocks, among frozen slime and the queasy comforts of the less vascular plants. It was a perfectly easy scramble but for the verglas. And the Doctor had tricounis. He loved them. Their toothless gums gnashed gallantly of his youth. 'Much more reliable than vibrams. Especially on ground like this. Now where' — fixing severely the interjecting Apprentice — 'where would crampons be on ground like this?' We agreed that, on ground like this, we did not know where crampons would be. So the Doctor had led off, scraping pointedly, impressing the moss, while we slid and clutched behind, nimble in fleeting soles. The angle had steepened, to frozen turf, enamelled slabs, and then these lounging blocks. So we had roped up, and the Doctor went on.

That was twenty minutes ago, and there had been no further medical bulletin. The Apprentice gazed about morosely, iron-less. His Wellington Street hoard was at home. This was only a loosening-up, and he had come — like me — because of the Doctor's car and considerate habits at bars on the way back.

The blocks eyed us genially, winking with an occasional fleck of snow. Still silence. 'Pull the bloody rope,' suggested the Apprentice. I pulled, quite hard. Shortly after, an irate tug indicated distant displeasure.

'Go up and see,' suggested the Apprentice. I moved off.

'I'll come, too,' said the youth. 'I'll stop you if you slip,' he added generously.

We acknowledged the boulders, patted the liverworts, and progressed slowly, scolding the little ropes as they ran into holes and behind spikes. At the top of a long sleeping block we met the Doctor, folded in a niche.

'Well, you're up at last,' he said. 'Not bad, for vibrams. Now wait here and I'll go on again.'

We persuaded him it would be quicker and safer to move together. Darkness and snow were approaching arm in arm, chanting on the wind. To please him we retained the twins, but whipped them into temporary obedience. If we slipped, the thoughtful blocks would sooner or later remember to stop us.

We reached the top of the heap. A few more gaping jumps, and then the greasy plates of summit scree, already well floured. And then, of course, he stuck.

'My foot!' he shouted.

It was well in, out of sight, between the last two big snoring blocks. The Apprentice and I pulled and pushed without avail. We beat thinly at tons of granite. Snow chilled our hands. Wind blew down our necks, telling us so.

Hoods up, we regarded the Doctor. He wiped slush from his eyes.

'Blast,' he remarked.

'Well, you can't stop here,' said the Apprentice. 'You'll have to get the boot off, or the bloody foot or something.'

He produced a large bowie-knife, looked enquiringly at the prisoner, who wiped away more snow, and then he poked it down, sharp end first, beside the ankle.

'Mind my foot.'

'It's the laces first, anyway.'

But he dropped the knife. It clattered irrecoverably.

'We'll have to make a sort of tent,' said the Doctor, 'anoraks weighed down with stones. And I'll be the pole.'

He was most brave. But it was nearly dark and the snow was that thick felted horizontal kind that means to get you. He had to come out. So we pulled, wrenched, back-broke him, until the startled knot peered up; fortunately the laces had been white. My penknife sawed away. A pencil worked under the tip of the tongue.

'Now pull yourself out of the boot.'

He lay back, contracting intensely, remembering the correct muscles.

Astonishingly — he was out. The boot dropped hollowly within. We fumbled at various darknesses for it, but it was well boxed. He hopped, cursing. We all cursed, gratefully. With oaths and a lace we bound a scarf round the outraged sock and led him off, but not before he'd scratched a mark on the impassive pedal sarcophagus, so that he could come back later with a crowbar.

We hirpled, baby nylons riding our shoulders, over the ridge on the tide of the night, and down rough soft leeward slopes to the eventual road, the blizzard singeing past into tall heather. We fell and rolled and were merry. The Apprentice found a torch in his sack, and it lit. Every flickering burn or so we tied up the scarf, wringing it out. But the foot was warm, thrilled with importance.

'A remarkable thing,' said the Doctor. 'In thirty years on the hills, it's never happened before. And they were going so well, far better than your vibrams. I suppose it was almost a Route. Do you know,' he said, 'I think we should call it The Clam.'

9

A Cave Meet

'The original Cave Meet,' explained the Doctor, 'was nothing of the sort. It was merely named after the cave Adullam, where the discontented gathered — in the twenty-second chapter of the first book of Samuel — remember? Chaps who disagreed with the Committee's Meet went to the Cave Meet, and climbed the hills they wanted to. What I'm suggesting' — he beamed round the silently-sipping table — 'is a Real Cave Meet. Speleology. Pot-holing.'

'Sort of climbing underground,' mused the Apprentice.

'Exactly. But you climb down to start off and up to come back.'

The Doctor was beginning to elaborate on the trials and rewards of the pursuit, when the bell rang. We resisted further attempts to raise our enthusiasm below ground level and left him at the Mound somewhat discouraged. 'But he'll be up to something soon, you bet, about these caves,' prophesied the Apprentice gloomily. 'We'll need to keep our weekends booked.'

Not until the Spring did caves rear themselves again. The Doctor drove us to the North-West for the May Holiday. We each designed one of the three days. The Apprentice forged us a new route on An Teallach for Saturday; I shepherded a Sunday marathon to Seana Bhraigh; and the Doctor had charge of Monday.

'An early start,' he warned, the night before. 'We've to drive a bit, first.'

The early start caused our first incident. The Apprentice,

eager to assist, offered to move the Doctor's car back to the road while we dismantled the tent. Unfamiliar with the early morning habits of the usually goodnatured old Mercedes, he was rather rough on the rein. Also he had forgotten that reverse occupied that particular position. The Doctor and I escaped with our lives; but the tent was less nimble.

'New poles,' concluded the Doctor philosophically, amidst beetroot apologies. 'We can eat at a B & B tonight. There's one near the place. Old MacGillivray's.'

Where the 'place' was and what we would do there he did not divulge. He hummed to himself, and our hearts sank. Still, it was his day; and it had been his tent. We kept silence.

We kept silence even when he stopped beside a cottage somewhere in Assynt, miles from anywhere above 500 metres. We kept silence when, with broad smiles, he pulled an old kitbag from the boot, loosened the strings and shook out an evil-looking heap of overalls and strange equipment.

The Apprentice automatically kneeled to examine the ironware. Certain items — pitons, slings, étriers, we recognised. But the rest . . .

The Doctor was proud of his Surprise.

'Ha, thought you'd be interested. Kept it a secret. In England over the New Year — why I wasn't at the Meet. Stayed with a friend at Ingleborough. He's a potholer. Taught me the drill. We did some fine things. Lost John. Alum Pot. And this is the best place in Scotland for caves. Unexplored. Don't worry. I'll lead. You just do exactly as you're told. Easy, for a climber. For instance, these wires . . . '

And he explained — clearly, I admit — the use of the more comprehensible pieces of iron and webbing. Miners' helmets. Carbide lamps. Flints. Kitbags. Pulleys. And an assemblage of neoprene holes graphically described as a 'wet-suit'.

Some of the kit was all too familiar.

'A shovel — a bloody shovel!' exclaimed the outraged Apprentice, holding up a trenching tool. The crowbar, short, black and malevolent, reduced him to silence.

'Might need 'em,' explained the Doctor. 'Unknown ground. Might have to assist Nature.'

Behind the car we changed into unyielding garb smelling of
the Ordovician. The Apprentice chose the wet-suit, covering
its widespread indecencies with pieces of overall. Unlike our
ragged selves the Doctor looked impressive. A Stakhanovite
face worker. His carbide, for example, slipped into his headlamp. We others trailed unhappy tubes from a bulging pocket.
'Yes, sometimes they do get caught.'

As he buttoned up, the Doctor began briskly extolling the
caves of the neighbourhood. He was becoming intolerable.

'And there's one by Inchnadamph, lived in just after the
Ice Age. Peach and Horne found lots of bones there — '

'Red deer, cave bear, reindeer-wolf-and-lynx,' intoned the
Apprentice. Cruel; but effective. The Doctor nodded, and
laced up his great ironclad boots. Silence.

We were ready. We became aware of prickling eyes of
children. Our leader looked at his watch.

'I'll go in and arrange supper,' he said. 'They do a damned
good meal.'

He emerged and beckoned us. Embarrassed, we creaked
in. Low ceiling. Spread table. More children.

We could not refuse the proffered cups. It was still not
nine o'clock.

Mrs MacGillivray, a large and capable body apparently
related to people who had looked after the Doctor's wife
when a child, doubted the pleasure our mission was supposed
to afford.

'And what would you be doing, down there away from the
sun and the air, on a fine day like this?' (What, indeed.)

Old MacGillivray, cleaning his gun in the corner, could not
see the *use* of it at all, at all. Though it might be interesting,
interesting. Down there. But *he* would not go. At all, at all.

Two of our hearts warmed to the MacGillivrays. But the
Doctor, rescuing a lump of carbide from a MacGillivray child
(they infested the place), enlarged upon the utility of the
pursuit. It appeared necessary to investigate almost every
crack in the ground, to see where it led . . . whether chambers,
cathedrals, lakes or rivers lay hidden beneath an innocent
sheep-snoring brae. Especially rivers.

'Your water will be hard, Mrs MacGillivray? I thought so. Good for thrombosis, bad for soap. And you say you sometimes run short? Well, potholers have often improved water supplies like yours — traced 'em right back, diverted other underground streams to feed 'em. Yours'll be fed by underground streams.'

The MacGillivrays' water supply, in fact, issued biblically out of a split rock just behind the house. Interest having been aroused, the Doctor dilated on the remarkable habits of underground rivers, popping into and out of holes like rabbits; even disappearing on one side of a mountain range, to reappear on the other.

We again became impatient, but old MacGillivray laid down his gun. Unfortunately, he was the ideal listener.

'And what way, Doctor, are they telling if it is the *same* water that comes out one side of a hill that goes in at the other?'

'Fluorescein, Mr MacGillivray, fluorescein. A green dye. A little lasts a long time, and goes a long way. Empty some in a burn one side of a hill — and look for green rivers on the other.'

'Then maybe they could be telling us where the Uisge Dubh comes from.'

The Uisge Dubh was the biggest river on the estate. Its salmon fishing was old Inverludie's main source of income. But it often fell very low, almost to dryness. Especially this year. Now *it* came out of a hole, way up in Coire Ghlas. Would *we* be able to trace its origin? No green dye, though — or very little. The fishing tenants might object.

'Perfectly harmless. But I see their point. Could dye the fish. Green salmon and salad . . . '

We brightened. The day achieved an aim. We would search for the underground source of the Uisge Dubh. McGillivray assured us the hole was big enough to squeeze through. Our clothes were old ones. And the Doctor was long, not wide. A fine opportunity, with the water so low. But it would be dangerous in rain. We would need a sharp eye in case the weather turned cloudy.

We reflected that the eye would need to be sharp to penetrate several hundred feet of Beinn a' Ghrunnda, a morose protruberance above the corrie which doubtless somewhere fathered the Uisge Dubh. Still, a touch of peril would add interest .. .

We trudged away, MacGillivray at the gate remarking that the weather might well hold. But he would not like to be going down there; at all, at all. But we should be doing a grand job, a grand job. The higher the Uisge Dubh the higher the fishing rent, and the higher the fishing rent the longer old Inverludie could keep The Company from buying up the estate.

The sight of the Hole silenced the Apprentice's harangue on Historical Necessity. It was indeed uninviting. Its waistcoat of grass was a poisonous emerald. It looked narrow enough, but by the end of the day we considered it well into the coach and horses category. It was, however, only three feet high, one of which feet was occupied by the Uisge Dubh.

'Light up!' cried the Doctor.

We worked our flints assiduously. At length a pallid glare appeared, flickering balefully as we soothed our tubes. The Doctor turned a knob, and immediately shone like Pharos. 'These later types are much better.'

With a sigh, the Apprentice and I knelt — Lord! — and squeezed into cold issuing darkness. The Doctor dismissed the few clouds in the west as insignificant, and followed. Why he didn't go first, I don't know. These things just happen. So we all had to back out again, cursing and bumping. Then he led in. I blinked furtively westward. Quite a few more clouds. Rushes were bending. South-west wind . . .

In again. I need not describe the progress. We were on all fours, straddled amongst vindictive boulders, in a foot of impatient elbowing water, kitbags clutching the roof. The Doctor's boots were just in front of my helmet, mine just in front of the Apprentice's. We suffered the basic principles of shunting. Clang. Stop. Clang. Go. Clang. Stop. Then cries from behind. The Apprentice's light had gone out. I turned my head; to be clouted back by the roof. Then mine went out. The carbide tin fell into the water.

In this emergency the light in front also disappeared. I roared. An echo. Then the Doctor's voice, booming Plutonically.

'Marvellous. Good Lord. Had no idea. Look at this!'

I bumped on towards the voice. A dim circle of light. I fell through, into a vast cavern, lit by the Doctor's headlamp. The luxury of — ah! — unfolding, standing up.

Preceded by oaths, the Apprentice appeared. He gazed up from the hole, chimpanzee-like. It really was remarkable. The air was still, warm. Only drips in the silence. Huge damp encrusted walls swam above us out of torchlight.

I wandered off across the pebbly beach, but was called back.

'Careful. Must keep together. Like a plateau in mist. Even Pitfoulie couldn't find us here.'

The Uisge Dubh itself had disappeared. Before hunting it, the Doctor took out compass, wax pencil and plastic notebook, and muttered and scribbled. We gathered it was much more difficult than back-bearings on Braeriach. He pencilled a runic symbol over the exit from our hole, then, nose down, bloodhounded the deepest centimetres of water, lifting his pencil intermittently to the nearest wall. We followed, the Apprentice occasionally adding artistic touches, for the pleasure of a future Abbé Breuil.

The cave unrolled, became narrower. At one point the Apprentice tweaked my sleeve, grinning. He extracted a huge meat bone from his kitbag (begged from Mrs MacGillivray, a woman with an iron sense of humour) and laid it by a boulder. It should interest the Doctor on the way back . . .

Presently we heard a thunder of splashing. The Apprentice paled beneath his acetylene. Those clouds.

'Ha, a waterfall. Thought so. Should make a good climb.'

Let us pass briefly over the next four hours. The three pitches in the waterfall (where the Apprentice's wet-suit acted like the rose on a watering can). The time the étrier stuck in the pulleys. The number of times the lights went out. The spilling of the spare carbide tin inside the Apprentice's wet kitbag, and his malodorous and potentially explosive presence thereafter. The contortions, abrasions, suffocations. The terrible thought of the sun above. The worse thought of the clouds.

Once, when we had come through a particularly trying tunnel, we were walking gratefully towards a flat clean floor and the Doctor was explaining the doubtless perinatal basis of our satisfaction ('Just like being born, you know'); when suddenly he disappeared and the floor parted in a splash.

'Should have remembered,' he spluttered. 'Still water's quite invisible.' This pleased us; until the pool ended in a blank wall. Below it the water lay black and faintly stirring. Horrible.

'Ah, a Sump. Good!'

The sump fulfilled its unattractive name. One had to go down under the oily water, along a short submerged passage (if there was one) and up to the other side (if, again, there was one). It was debatable who would fare worse – the leader seeking a way, or the last man, alone with thoughts of the Other Side.

The Doctor probed. He knelt, dipped his head and rubber torch. We watched these more veterinary procedures numbly. His head emerged.

'Looks all right. Quite short. What luck to find one. Superb cave. Now, you hold on to this string. It's tied to me. I'll tug twice when I'm through. Three times and you follow. Don't get tangled in it.' And he disappeared completely.

The water gurgled, and resumed its black ruminations. The Apprentice squatted glumly, holding his string. We counted and watched the line. A float would have helped. Ten. Twenty. No bite. Fifty. A hundred . . . We looked at each other. 'Tug it,' I suggested.

He tugged. No reply. He pulled, and the string rose, length after length, from the darkness, to the very end. We laid it reverently on the muddy bank, a wet wreath. Well . . .

'We've *got* to find him . . . !' – and the Apprentice, too, slipped down and vanished into the unknown.

My feelings may be imagined. Five. Ten. Twenty . . . Suddenly the water boiled and a gasping Apprentice appeared. 'He's trapped, struggling,' he choked, and vanished again. Sweat. Ages. Then another swirl, and the Apprentice emerged, dragging a convulsive figure after him. We stretched the wreckage on the bank, coughing and streaming. The Apprentice's remarkable courage had been rewarded. He smiled modestly. I gripped his hand.

When sufficiently oxygenated, the Doctor sat up. (He had violently refused the Kiss of Life.) He swore. Loudly, and for half a minute. We feared shock. But it was not shock. The explanation panted out, punctuated by fearsome hoastings and spittings.

He had got to the other side. But the string had come undone. He had waited. No follower. So he had plunged in again and gone back in search. Midway in the submerged tunnel he had encountered the Apprentice — also in search. Naturally they vigorously attempted to rescue each other. Neither won, and each retired to his corner for air. In the second round, as we had seen, the Apprentice prevailed.

After a decent interval, the Doctor led off again, *sans* string. It was bad, but soon over. The Doctor wrung my hand, adjusted my trembling helmet.

'Jolly good, eh? Don't worry' — as my shakings increased — 'I've a CO_2 lifejacket, in case you get cramp.'

That lifejacket nearly belied its name, as we shall see. But just then we guests were quite demoralised. The Apprentice was praying for the elevated peace of a *sestogrado*.

'Blood glucose low. Good spot for a bite.' So we ate our acetylene sandwiches, by one lamp turned down. The Doctor, munching, peered at his muddy pages, tapped his fingers mathematically. Navigation was in progress.

'We should be almost at the watershed, if the strata lie as I think. That means we *could* divert the next big stream we meet. It's through that wall, probably,' — indicating a brutal million tons or so — 'and send it down the one we've come up. *That* would feed the Uisge Dubh, and buck up old Inverludie no end.'

We pointed out that despite the pleasure of old Inverludie we had to get out by the hole we came in, together with old Inverludie's increased rental.

'Of course, we first need to find a higher way out. But there are dozens of little passages up there. Shouldn't take long.'

With foreboding, we climbed after him. Three wax pencils and a ball of string later, navigation assured us we were on tapping terms with the southwest face of Beinn a' Ghrunnda. As if to confirm this improbable suggestion, a hairline of light coincided in all our imaginations at the end of a tunnel on the right. But that tunnel was even narrower than ours. We stuck. Retreat throttled us with jackets.

'No good. Have to strip off,' said the Doctor.

'Strip off?'

'Put clothes in kitbags and drag 'em behind.'

This last degradation was not eased by the Doctor's jovially clinical remarks. He led off. I followed his kitbag. Then my kitbag. Then the Apprentice. Then, presumably, his kitbag. The Doctor gripped the trenching tool. ('Might need it; but mustn't dislodge anything; could be awkward.')

After an hour and twenty feet of this horizontal crux, even our leader became less sanguine. With weary humour the Apprentice suggested we call it off and get back before they missed us at roll-call. Kitbags mercifully fielded the Doctor's subsequent puns about Stalag Meit. Then he called excitedly.

'I can dig here. I'm sure there's light ahead. We're moving.' Then, 'My kitbag's jammed. Poke it along and I'll pull with my foot.'

I poked. He pulled. Badly jammed. The crowbar in it didn't help. Pull. Push. It moved a little, then hooked once more.

In despair I punched it, hard into its guts. Damn the thing.

Then a hiss. Carbide? Good Lord, not here.

Not carbide. No smell. But the bag began to bulge, expand, swell visibly, until it filled the whole width of the passage. It was quite immovable, and resilient as a football.

Communication with the Doctor became understandably even more difficult, but I gathered that I must have depressed the emergency button on the CO_2 lifejacket. It was now inflated, and would keep the wearer afloat for 4 weeks in a normal sea.

'Jings!' said the Apprentice, when informed. He reserved mildest oaths for the worst occasions. I agreed. We simply had to uncork the Doctor. We caterpillared back, propelling our bags. In the relative space of the outer passage we searched them for suitable instruments. Then the Apprentice — he was fresher, and this was clearly a V.S. pitch — went in, a great knife between his teeth and a hook (probably meant for some shuddering abseil) in his hand. I squatted and tried to keep warm and think of nothing. Especially not of CO_2 poisoning. *Grotte des Chiens.*

At last a scuffling, gasping. The operation had been successful. Breech delivery. The Doctor lay, deflated as his kitbag. But we had to get back. While we dressed he admitted that although there must be an exit along there, this perhaps was not the time to explore it. Rheumatically, we returned, ticking off the waxings, winding up the string. Before the sump, the Doctor made a half-hearted sortie; but he could not go far alone . . . We others pointedly pricked our jets.

He crawled back, jubilantly. He had found two small streams. One on the right should be the Uisge Dubh; the other, its potential feeder. To gain information, he had put a little — just a little — fluorescein into the left-hand one. In a cardboard packet. So as not to get ourselves all green, if it did happen to be the Uisge Dubh. The cardboard would dissolve in a couple of hours, when we should be out.

We made good time. The sump held no terrors. We had less clothes and skin to delay us in the tunnels. The Doctor, leanest, was well ahead. Suddenly he bellowed

'CAVE BEAR!'

Thirty thousand years of conditioning flung myself and the Apprentice high up the wall. We clung there a horrible second before contemporary sense and the Doctor returned, the latter dangling Mrs MacGillivray's bone.

'Ha!' he said.

The Apprentice, higher than I was, carefully concluded his examination of an interesting section of strata. We climbed down and continued.

Fast. Faster. We wanted sun and air. Even the Doctor claimed he smelt grass (*Molinia*). We worried about the clouds. But our leader had recorded the drips per second at various spots on the way in; as the same number dripped on the way out, he pronounced it still a fine day.

It was. Two hours later we lay on the bank, photosynthesising morale. The water showed no trace of dye, then or as we staggered down to the cottage.

'That left-hand branch will make a fine feeder. We'll come back' — he caught our eyes — '*I'll* come back with that Ingleborough chap and switch the points. Then old Inverludie can enjoy his moths in peace.' (The laird was a diligent lepidopterist; he had taken a Dotted Footman on the very slopes we were crossing.) The Uisge Dubh had more or less washed us and the sun had dried us. We changed at the car.

Weary, almost happy, certainly very relieved, we plodded up MacGillivray's path. An urchin scampered down, swinging two yellow buckets. Birds sang.

'Well, and did you enjoy your day?' Mrs MacGillivray, arms akimbo, looked quizzically down at us. We truthfully said it had been memorable. The Doctor limped over to old MacGillivray; he began to sketch and explain vigorously.

'Your supper will be a little late,' said Mrs MacGillivray. 'I've had to send the lad out for water. But there's enough for you to wash,' she added, a trifle grimly. She returned to the kitchen.

The Apprentice looked at his hands and guessed about his face. Also, he still smelt a little. He went to the bathroom. I patted a small wetnosed child.

Suddenly a roar. The Apprentice's head through the doorway. It was a horrible colour of bile. I leapt up. Acetylene poisoning . . .

'Green! The water's all green!'

The Doctor spun round in horror.

'Green! All green!' the Apprentice roared.

Mr MacGillivray went on talking.

'I would not like to have been down there at all, at all,' he said.

10

Fixing us Up
(The Dreepie)

The forecast was frightful for the North. Gale winds, blizzards of powder snow. Gullies would be choked, faces wiped. All this after weeks of rain, and now in a final pipe-splitting frost. And the Apprentice had brand-new lobster-points to try out, cooked expensively to a gourmet's taste, and I a grinning Terrordactyl of advanced evolution, fierce from its creator; both of us fondled virgin ice-daggers fit for some sub-glacial Mafia. We had lightened our wallets for the new season, and this could have been the first run. We ached to prickle up some crisp verticality, glassy between admiring cliffs. We thought of Zero in two hours. We were bitter . . .

So we fell for the Doctor's jovial invitation:

'I can fix you up!'

He would take us to some southern ice. Not the Lakes — weather just as bad there. Nor even the Grey Mare's Tail — that would fairly wag in this wind. But much nearer:

'Just outside Edinburgh — edge of the Moorfoots. Perfect just now — sheltered, private, fine for a practice.'

Our forebodings, well-nourished on the past, gorged themselves as we trudged up the scabby grass of vast mounds ambling with sheep. But no: improbably, two of these heaps heaved back and exhibited, with considerable pride, an astonishingly high and apparently vertical earthern gully. On either side grazed well-belayed sheep; below lay more earth, and more sheep; but within, a sliver of ice launched dazzlingly upwards to a giddy bulge and then vanished backwards into blue sky.

The Doctor extended a long arm hospitably: 'This hill's the Corse o' Whalloch, and that's — Whalloch's Dreepie. It should fix you up all right.'

Apparently the Dreepie only dreeped after heavy rain, being fed from a bog above. Some geological quirk ensured its almost vertical incision in turfy earth.

We approached gingerly and prodded. The surface was yielding but sound; inside was hard.

'It's even better higher up,' announced our host complacently.

We demurred a little at the grass stems, rushes and bits of turf poking through here and there.

'Ah, they give it body. Make it tough, absolutely reliable. Can't come away. Never splits. Make it like fibreglass, reinforced concrete, bricks with straw; and all that.'

We cut short the Doctor's technical explanations of Griffith cracks and buckled on our new equipment. The Doctor was faithful to long axe, fishing hat, tweeds and tricounis. 'You can hold a long axe short, but not a short one long.' And tweeds stuck better than terylene — but, he assured us, the Dreepie ice would be very adherent.   It was.

He took to the proffered lead ('Might as well show the way') and bucketed up at a showering Charlet gallop. Earth and roots, as well as ice, fell around us. Unconvinced by the stems, we had agreed on a rope. We hoped only sheep were watching. Our leader hacked a platform, harrowed it, and summoned us.

The Apprentice went before me, taking the thin unbucketed edge, pointing elegantly. I followed, loops in hand. It was good stuff. A gentle kick and a stab: delicious admittance, firm grasp. Wonderfully safe. We mounted rapidly, calves thrilling. Marvellous to be back on ice — even if the Nordwand of a Corse o' Whalloch and ten feet wide, and even if sheep did munch mildly eye to eye with you as you passed. *Maa.* We were merry, and exchanged a word with each of them in turn. *Baa.*

The Doctor, having identified for us the local Traverse of the Gods and the White Spider (the latter carrying much grass in its web), began the final stretch below the bulge.

'Time me. See how much longer you are with spikes. No need for crampons in Scotland — take all the craft out of climbing. And as for daggers — too damned emotional.'

Multi-coloured débris rocketed past: the Apprentice drove in a peg to make sure, extracted his claws with difficulty and then slammed them well home; we would cut no steps. I did likewise, some 15ft. below, and we settled to wait, muscles twanging. But it was good training for the Ben and Raven's and the rest.

The Doctor's toothy heels above us ceased to gnash: 'Come on up a bit. I'll need all the rope to get over that bulge.'

The Apprentice nodded, unclipped and heaved at his peg, cursed, bashed it, heaved and cursed again. Jammed fast.

'Ah, that's the Dreepie ice,' explained the Doctor. 'Particularly near the edge. It's the mud and stems. Plastic. Very binding.   Leave it for now.'

The Apprentice cursed again, straightened up and tried to extract his left foot. Squirm.

His right foot. Squirm.

His dagger. Squirm.

He undulated on his points of attachment like a tent in a gale. But he did not take off. He was stuck.

Stuck.

Terrible oaths. Squirm,

Stuck . . .

I informed our consultant.

'It'll be the grass again. Same as for the peg. Still, it does make it absolutely reliable . . . Pity you *had* to use those things. Rather spoilt a classic little climb. Shouldn't have kicked in so far; but then of course you mightn't have kicked in far enough . . . Need plenty of experience, crampons. Especially in Scotland.'

We decided to abandon the Apprentice meanwhile. I was to unclip the rope, reach the Doctor, and belay him. Then he could top the bulge, gain the bog, peg in, abseil down and prise our writhing companion from his flypaper.

'You just wait there,' the Doctor called down, 'you'll be fine, you can't fall; Dreepie ice is very firm . . .'

It had begun to snow. I was fortunately below the really possessive stuff. I clawed up the steps. The Doctor then tackled the bulge.

The ice went *poop* under his axe. He explained how to carve such rubber. He feathered his slash ('like rowing Stroke in rough water'), then spooned each step backwards adze-wise ('like serving jelly; but firmer').

Much firmer. I found my prongs tight. I kicked back in alarm. But I must have offended some monocotyledon or other, for my left foot shot free and swung me backwards out of balance. I flung up both arms and my Terrordactyl took wing. I saw the Doctor silhouetted above, tongue out, reaching his axe over the bulge. With a fearful effort I lunged forward again on my right foot and drove the dagger well home before me; and clung. Relief. Sob.

But I had stabbed the rope and buried it through the dagger point well into the solid treacle.   Irretrievable . . .

And worse . . . Groans from above indicated that I had tautened the rope just as my leader had fully extended himself and his tongue, arm over the bulge. He had been pulled down onto his tongue and his angular chin, his axe had been driven in hard somewhere up there and his grip plucked off it; so that his bony wrist now flapped weakly above, twisted firmly into the end of the axe-sling.

We were indeed in a fix; in a frozen frieze. Snow fell heavier, burying the Doctor's bitten and fragmentary oaths. The sheep were impressed. They crowded the top of The Dreepie, chewing knowledgeably. Then they scattered. They had been disturbed. We heard other voices:

'Aye, aye; ye'll be daein an ice-climb.'

'That'll be hit: they'll be daein an ice-climb!'

A miracle. Geordie and Wull. Two inveterate veteran hill-bashers, cautious in all weathers. They masticated their jammy pieces above us, brushing snow off their balaclavas.

'Ye'll soon be there, lads. Hang on. There's naethin after this,' said Geordie.

'Aye, it ends here,' confirmed Wull. 'Stick tae it.'

They consulted each other for a moment, crust to crust.

'A pity ye couldna stop like yon for jist a bittie longer; for the ithers tae see ye,' suggested Geordie, through crumbs. 'If yer holds is good, mind.'

'Aye, they'd like fine tae see yese hack-hackin yir way up,' added Wull. 'Jist stay there, like, if ye can.'

It appeared that Geordie and Wull were but the van of a whole flutter of local sub-Munroists, the Pittemdoon Cairn Gatherers, who, like us, had been deterred from going north and had swooped on the Corse o' Whalloch as suitable low-level carrion for their day.

We tried to explain, gurgles above and expletives beneath, our predicament, now truly horrendous. But Geordie and Wull were slow, and voices began to chirrup above us. O the shame, shame of it . . . I glimpsed orange anoraks and peering eyes. I felt cameras being unpacked, lenses screwed on.

But Geordie was not that slow. He had his own camera in his hand, a huge mahogany box-like affair, and fixed his brassy tripod. Then he waved the others back, flourishing a jammy piece:

'Awa, awa. I'm takin a verra careful shot of thae lads, an I want a clear background. Awa, all o ye, now!'

'Groogh,' agreed the Doctor through an ice-and-tongue sandwich under his immovable neck. 'We can't, oorgh, stay here, grrgh, like this all, urrgh, damned day.'

'Aye,' added Wull, catching on. 'These lads wants awa, they're no verra firm whaur they are. Hurry on doon tae yir bus, there's mair snaw comin in.' And he drove them off, breathing heavy experience.

Well, eventually they extricated us. It was a long job, for they were careful, gey careful, and every step they cut along the horizontal frozen bog (of course they had brought their axes) had to be brushed out and tested several times and their rope (of course they had brought their rope) had to be tied and untied several times and tugged and pondered over and discussed repeatedly; but by evening — and another couple of inches of snow — they had released the Doctor's axe, watched wonderingly our subsequent excruciating and arthritic manoeuvres, had rubbed us down and had helped us carry back the various blocks of mud and ice impounding our gear (we dared not chip too close). We thanked them with the bottle of Glen Reechie the Doctor had brought for our celebration, and watched them pack it away unopened in their van. As they left, Geordie promised to send us a print of the picture he had taken: 'It would be a better reproduction, like, than the one we would see in the *Journal*.'

'A fine climb, The Thweepie, in itthway,' concluded the Doctor over his mutilated tongue as we drove stiffly off. 'Hardly the Bwenva, or even Minuth One or Pawallel B, but gwand for exerthithe; and for teaching you thomethin about Thcottith Ithe.'

Behind the back seat, the glaciers — and their accompanying moraines — retreated silently from our 39 points into his — fortunately — open rucksack.

11

A Yacht Meet

It was not long after the unfortunate episode of the Cave
Meet, and we should have learned to leave the nineteenth
century alone. The Doctor was reading out of a recent Club
Journal, carefully keeping its pages above the spirituous rings
of the table in Daddy McKay's.

' . . . that supreme Victorian event, the Yacht Meet of
1897, and the desperate race back off Sgùrr na Ciche before
the Presidential Yacht sirened finality and sailed away down
the loch . . . Whisky in the panelled smoking room and piping
on the after-deck, with the sun setting over Skye beyond the
loch and the President dancing a reel . . . '

'There,' said the Doctor. 'That's what we should have. A
Yacht Meet.'

'Lies,' pronounced the Apprentice, who had suspicions of
that particular *Journal* editor. 'Lies. He made it all up.
Always did. Even invented his contributors. The biggest liar
out.'

The Doctor defended the now retired office bearer, though
he looked thoughtful. Several of his own articles ('the best
ones, too') had suffered editorial Improvement.

'No,' concluded the Doctor, 'it's perfectly true. It's described away back in volume four, in 1898. We should do
something like it now. Trouble is, who has a boat big enough
these days?'

We thought. 'Macassar?' suggested the Apprentice.

'Lord, yes! Of course, Macassar! He has several, by all

accounts. And his place is just by the very loch . . .'

On the next Thursday we were informed that arrangements were complete. The Doctor had phoned, and had been answered favourably. A large ocean-going motor yacht, complete with crew and stateroom, lay at our disposal for the following weekend. All we had to do was drive over. It sounded most attractive. I put off a visit south and the Apprentice, to the amazement of his fellow-Weasels, forewent a promising line on the Ben — *Wedgewood*, a little to the left of *Sassunach*. Early on the Saturday morning we were cantering along a West Highland road in the Doctor's old Mercedes. We discussed our benefactor.

Sir Hector Macassar was, by universal agreement, a remarkable man. Unanimity stopped there. The Doctor had known him as a student, and had climbed with him in the J.M.C.S. Even at that age the youth had organised things — bus meets, expeditions abroad, convenient loans. With the greatest breeze and aplomb he had risen in the world, by means that no one — not even the Doctor — understood. There were hints, of course; but doubtless prompted by envy. The Macassar expeditions became world-famous, his films and books universally applauded. That description of how he sank a pursuing polar bear with his canoe paddle had been translated into a dozen languages. Both Poles he knew, the Himalayas and every big range in the world. Amazonian jungles, remote Polynesian islands, world-renowned political figures. For some of these activities — which ones were not divulged, but rumour included two international business men, a hundred thousand dollars and an ex-Prime Minister — he had been knighted. Yet he remained essentially the same Macassar as in youth, jovial and unpretentious. The motto above his arms read *Faill ill o agus ho ro eile*, and only cynics regarded this as his considered comment. He kept close connections with the Club and established the Macassar Trust; this presented emulators, if their expeditions had been successful, with a medal showing himself on both sides and offered them a complete set of his books, fully illustrated and at reasonably reduced prices.

Such was the man whose estates we were now approaching. Invercannilie Castle, an enormous Victorian pile, had belonged to an admiring reader of his, a rich old lady. Sir Hector had naturally returned the admiration, and had been duly bequeathed the castle and a few thousand acres. As the rich old lady's next-of-kin employed counsel unversed in the balance holds of Scottish law, he had remained there, and now held court in Renaissance splendour. Or so we had been told. We waited dry-mouthed for our first glimpse of Invercannilie.

Our first glimpse was a huge signboard and a menagerie of shanties — *Invercannilie Caravan Park*. Sir Hector was a well-known environmentalist. To prevent the coastline (previously inaccessible) from being overrun by Sporadic Development, he had constructed a road and this park. Sportingly, he had built it on his own land. The inmates appeared suitably subdued and the charges not unduly excessive.

Beyond the caravans, a high wall and gates. We were admitted, somewhat doubtfully, by the wifie at the lodge. Within, the grounds were peaceful. We dipped down to the loch. Through spires of *Sequoiadendron* we saw white-washed turrets, gleaming in the early sun. Above the highest flew Sir Hector's own flag. It much resembled that of the Bank of Scotland, but the *roundels, or,* were replaced by small golden cuboids. 'Liar Dice,' averred the Doctor. 'Sir Hector's favourite game.' Below it, on a smaller turret, flew the national flag, of the authentic azure. Sir Hector was a devoted patriot.

We crunched to a halt outside the main entrance, the Mercedes cringing on the half-acre of gravel. Impressed, we mounted several flights of steps. An attractive young lady of eastern appearance received us at the swing doors and ushered us into a huge vestibule. She took our names, and vanished.

'Do sit down' — another, equally attractive, young lady. We declined. We were, unashamedly, amazed. Invercannilie entrance hall had been vast enough to begin with, designed for some megalomaniac Victorian stockbroker. Its eighty-foot-high vaulted ceiling would accommodate smoke from several board-rooms of cigars. But Sir Hector had wonderfully increased its guest-humbling magnificence. Walls flaunted spears and harpoons, targes, totems and gongs. From the invisible ceiling hung sails, kayaks and outriggers. About the floor lay skins of half the larger *Mammalia*. Stuffed heads eyed us severely from every corner. It was easy to see, as the Apprentice remarked, that Sir Hector frequently took his holidays abroad. And all around, immense bustle, a tripping to and fro of attractive young ladies, mostly of exotic origin, carrying piles of papers.

'Secretaries,' explained the Doctor. 'They help in the house. Sir Hector has so little time. And now this Oil . . . '

A tremendous crash. The Apprentice, stepping back to admire a secretary, had tripped over the open muzzle of a rug and dislodged a complete set of *samoura-oura,* rare Amazonian blowpipes. They were fortunately not properly poisoned, and he was being reassured by a circle of secretaries when our names were called and we were led out of the hall, along a trilling conservatory bright with humming-birds and into a swift and silent lift. It deposited us on to a plush air-conditioned corridor. A door opened. A great hand extended.

'Wonderful to see you!'

Sir Hector was huge, bearded and beaming, in nondescript tweeds and a pink shirt. Waved to chairs, we listened as he leant back, boots on the desk among the telephones, and explained why he was sorry. Our yacht, it seemed, had already been booked. Only for this weekend. But by a *great* friend of his, the Emir of somewhere or other (Sir Hector's Arabic was too colloquial to follow). Visiting on business. And the Emir had only this week in Scotland, whereas we lived here. We would understand. We would be fair. Next weekend? The other big yachts — only five since that affair at Ekofisk — were hired out — were lent — all the summer, but this, the best, would be free next weekend.

None of us could face the build-up of another such day. Had he nothing else?

Sir Hector considered. He jumped up. A telephone fell.

'I'm sure we must have. But small, very small. Some of the girls go sailing. And we hire a few to caravanners. Let's go and look. You're sure you don't want a power boat? We've plenty of those. The boys love them. And old Donald Archie. They're great fun.'

The journey to the boats was memorable. Our host's breezy commentary on everything we passed, from Patagonian fire-sticks to a newly-installed computer console ('a prototype I got from the Mitsubishi people to try out here') dazed us. We were briefly introduced to Donald Archie, the head keeper. He was sitting on a stool at the swimming pool Coke bar, next to the jukebox. His eyes said nothing — with considerable emphasis.

Down at the quay floated a duckweed of small boats.

'Now, which would you like?'

They were all very small. The Doctor, who had brought his pipes to play on the after-deck at evening, gazed glumly at a snuggle of two-seater Mirrors. Sir Hector could not have been more helpful. He skipped, with ease long born of killer whales and icefloes, from bow to bow. We followed, skidding on fibreglass, clutching diminutive masts.

'Why, here's a trimaran. Didn't know we had one left. That's big enough. You could have a hull each.'

But we declined. They were chancy things, the Doctor said. We decided on a G.P.14. Fourteen feet. *An Sgarbh*. The Cormorant. It would just about be able to cram us all in.

'Excellent!' said Sir Hector.

We gazed wistfully offshore at the great glittering vessel that lay under the black sardonic mountains of Knoydart. Men ran about its decks, polished its white hull from cradles.

'You know,' said Sir Hector, 'I'm really sorry you can't have the *Mobaidh Dhic* this weekend. But any other time, remember, she's yours. Unless, of course, we have sudden guests. They all like a trip.' I avoided the Doctor's morose eye.

'Raeburn was a good sailor,' remarked the Doctor reassuringly from the helm as we battered up the loch. 'Damn,' he added. A large wave had stared in and jumped aboard. The wind was

increasing, gusting from the dark hanging glens above us.
Sgùrr na Ciche vanished ahead into mist. Waves broke white
on the shore we were making for. Our rucksacks were sodden.
We recalled that cormorants frequently travelled long dis-
tances underwater.   It was not very enjoyable.

The crew did their best. The Apprentice, despite twinges
of *samoura-oura*, leapt from gunwale to gunwale at our
skipper's command, leaning well out, at times half-immersed.
I held various ropes, sometimes dodging the boom, which
uncannily anticipated the Doctor's intentions. His subsequent
'Gybe ho!' was delivered apologetically, while the victim
groaned in the bilge.

Some thirty feet off shore, the inevitable happened. The
Sgarbh took the bit in its beak, and went for a dive. Despite
Sir Hector's lifejackets we swam fairly well and beached most
of our kit, including the distraught Doctor's pipes. Then we
beached the boat, well up on the silverweed. We wrung ourselves damp, and helped the Doctor wash and lay out his
reeds ('*just* blown in!'). Then lastly we plodded towards our
peak, trying to forget last night's anticipation of today, the
Apprentice gloomy with imagined Amazonian toxins.

It was a good peak, though, high and sharp above low
cloud. The cloud considerately hid the loch, the *Mòbaidh
Dhic* and the unrepentant *Sgarbh*. A large piece of seaweed,
found in the Apprentice's rucksack, was placed on the cairn,
to disturb the next Munroist. The Doctor added a crab's leg
from his pocket. In the sun we dried, convinced ourselves
we could see Ben Wyvis, and tried to forget the sail back. To
walk to the car would take too long, and would be discourteous. There was, moreover, the *samoura-oura* to be
humoured.

Halfway down we heard a curious noise. A wail. The
Doctor was furious. 'Some ass trying my pipes!' But the
wail continued, with a full-throated urgency no marinaded
reed could aspire to. It was so like a ship's siren. Unmistakably like.

We looked at each other, and misery returned. The irony.
Ah well. We dropped down through the cloud, despondent.

The cloud cleared. The siren roared. We saw the loch, slicing sunlit between Morar and Knoydart. And on it a white ship, just off-shore beneath us. Sirens again. And a power-boat running about ecstatically like a small dog. The Doctor pulled out his Trinovids, wiped off the salt, and gazed.

'Lord, it's the *Mòbaidh Dhic*. And there's Macassar in the speedboat. Pink shirt. What on earth . . . He's seen us. He's waving. Do you think . . . ?'

We did think. We ran, leaping hags and boulders, falling, floundering, to the motherly bellowings of the *Mòbaidh Dhic*.

That evening the Doctor piped indeed. On the after-deck. Not with his own set. The prawns were still in it. But with Sir Hector's gold-mounted Robertson's. As Sir Hector's piper was away at a wedding for that month, the Doctor played uninhibitedly. Fortified by a fine meal and much Glen Rauchle, we heard him in peace. Then Sir Hector had a blow. He played surprisingly well. 'Better than he used to,' remarked the Doctor, 'but it's the pipes, of course. A great thing, gold.' We danced a reel, unsteadily. Our host, the Emir, beamed among his attendants.

For the ship *had* been lent to the Emir. But Sir Hector's conscience, resilient as ever despite forty-odd years with its master, had whispered in His Eminence's ear. About our upset plans. And the Emir insisted on helping us out. He insisted, too, on a Blow. The three of us, Sir Hector, the Doctor and I, held his wavering instrument upright while the attendants raised their hands and marvelled and the drones roared farewell to the great sunset hills at the head of the loch, to Sgùrr na Ciche with its piece of seaweed and its crab's leg, and to the two MacDonalds and a MacRae who were trying, between drams, to hammer the centreboard back into *An Sgarbh*. The chanter, for its part, frequently managed to achieve low G.

The fourth of us, the Apprentice, was not on deck to appreciate this glorious consummation. Not because of the *samoura-oura*. Because of a secretary.

12

A Wet Day

'One should always,' said the Doctor, 'climb something on a wet day. Anything; so long as you get to the top. It gives the day a point.'

We lay in our bags, disagreeing at length. The Apprentice clinched his view by turning over and re-burying his head. It was the fifth day of rain, and we appreciated the Doctor's tent, massive in architecture and material. Warned by the forecast, we had helped to carry this edifice, improbably folded and in puffing sections, up from the old Mercedes. So that if our own more portable shelter should decide to admit the overwhelmingly liquid phase of a late Scottish October, we could with a dry conscience beg accommodation.

We had climbed, the first three days, hard rock, easy rock, and finally a stretch of bog elevated by Munro to undeserved eminence. The Apprentice and I had spent the night before last mopping about us with towels: toasting tent walls and edges of bags with an urgent primus; and squeezing ourselves further up the ever-diminishing non-tidal area of the ground-sheet. The Doctor's crowded *salon* was luxury to that. Why should we leave it?

The previous day, climbing had not even been suggested. Rain was heavy, our shirts were wet and the Doctor had decided to beat us at chess. He promised a new opening, to confound us. But it confounded him also, and I managed a draw; nor could all his beady-eyed craft and pipe-smoke preserve him from rout by the Apprentice's resolutely marching pawns. So we had veered towards music, the Doctor with his chanter, the Apprentice with his moothie; I had tried to read. A literally potted banquet — four courses in an alloy cauldron — occupied the remaining hours.

Yes, we were bored; but not that bored. The rain was still heavy. Even the ridge of the Doctor's tent, stitched from dinosaur hide, had softened to dampness at one corner; the flysheet, a melancholy kind of canvas mainsail, beat and wept on it continually. To go out on the hill would risk abandoning the only dry square inches in Argyll to penetration by a slowly-moving depression southwest of Iceland. Ridiculous.

Then the opening darkened. Voices.

'Ay, they're inside. On a day like this. Terrible.'

'They'll be wantin to keep out of the rain.'

'Verra likely.'

The Doctor extended an arm, and raised the flap higher. Drips shuddered from canvas on to flattened grass. Beyond, we saw two pairs of woolly-socked pillars, booted and gaitered, fit to support a Clydesdale. Two heads, moistily balaclava'd, bent down to join them; and peered in.

'Ha,' said the Doctor. They were a couple of wellknown heather-bashers, impervious to mist, rain, sleet, insult or lightning; and liable to be encountered on any undemanding mountain. They were referred to by all as Geordie and Wull. Both were heavily prudent, disliking rock, or snow above 10°. Wull was particularly cautious. He carried two of everything, just in case; maps, compasses, pairs of gloves, bootlaces, braces, primuses, even a spare rucksack — packed, somewhat illogically, within the other one; he should have hung them fore and aft.

'Come on out,' said Geordie.

Wull squatted in front of the door. He gleamed all over, moisture and wool, grey moustache, spectacles and both wrist watches.

'Don't stay in there,' he said.

The tedium of our surroundings was such that we greeted these worthies with interest, if scarcely with rapture. A temporary brightening of the sky, coupled with now three-fold urgings, lured the Apprentice and myself out of bags and into cold damp breeks and boots. We had already breakfasted, and the Doctor now spread pieces.

Meanwhile Geordie was inspecting the tent, tweaking the flysheet powerfully.

'A braw tent,' he concluded. 'Strong,' he added, leaning with all his weight on the front pole; 'gey strong', leaning equally unsuccessfully on the rear pole.

The Doctor grew more anxious to go. Geordie was a good thirteen stone, and liable to continue his inspection.

We were in fact ready to go, but Wull was still squatting at the doorway, staring benignly within.

We crowded the exit, pointedly.

'I'll be in your way, like,' admitted Wull, and hoisted himself up by the front guy. Geordie genially replaced the peg. 'A gey strong tent. No many like it the day.' He gave a final appreciative slap to the flysheet. The Doctor turned him about firmly, reinserted the rear peg and checked the rest of the rigging. We gathered, chilled and unhappy, in the resuming rain.

Where were we going?

'Come with us, lads,' suggested Geordie. 'We're doing Meall nan Adharc.' Meall nan Adharc? We hadn't heard of it. Hardly a peak, not even a Munro, not even a Top. Geordie explained: it was one of the Five Hundreds — a ghastly list of every Separate Mountain over 500 metres ('that's 1,650 feet', translated Wull), compiled by some besieged and lunatic extremist. Our visitors had of course done all the Munros and Tops within, and Furth Of, Scotland (Wull had done them twice, to make sure) and were well on the way to completing this lower débris; how many hundreds I cannot bear to recall.

'It's just another hump of bog.' We were sceptical.

'No, no' — Geordie and Wull rolled weighty glances at each other — 'it's *rocky* at the top. You lads'll like it fine. Mebbe you could look after us — eh? See we come to no harm?' 'Keep an eye on us, like?' added Wull. It is difficult to define the extent of − or the existence of − Geordie and Wull's sense of humour. Their smiling amplitude betrays no irony. Perhaps it *was* rocky. Perhaps they had, seeing the Doctor's car at the road, looked us up for this reason. They were always careful.

'Right-ho, we'll look after you, then,' cried the Doctor. We moved off. The Apprentice and I felt we were being imposed upon. Wull sidled up to us. 'You see, it's *rocky* at the top,' he confided. 'Nan Adharc means: of the horns.' Geordie overheard. 'That's right. Horns, you see. Rocky at the top. Nan Adharc. Of the horns.'

Not a rock for hours did we see. Peat hag after hag, imperceptibly higher, perceptibly wetter. Even the Doctor became subdued; his pipe, reserved for such occasions, went out. But Geordie and Wull stumped on through the mist, unperturbed. Wull took off his balaclava occasionally, mopped his brow and turned and gleamed at us (it was hot inside two cagoules − one cotton, one terylene), but never stopped. This was nothing to them. A good solid plod. Restful. They took bearings, double-checked by Wull.

'We'll soon be there,' said Geordie.

'Not long now,' added Wull.

Then we heard it. A deep roaring. Silence. And a roaring again, nearer.

'Stags,' said the Doctor, 'rutting. We're probably walking into somebody's territory.'

We continued. But Geordie and Wull exchanged glances again. They halted. Wull fumbled in his rucksack. He brought out mysterious packages and shared them with his companion. We looked, questioningly.

'It's stags,' said Geordie.

'Stags,' confirmed Wull.

Seeing our continued incomprehension, Geordie explained more fully. 'Paraffin on a rag; matches; pepper.' Our eyes widened further.

'For the stags,' he added.

'In case they attack,' said Wull.

They always carried these antidotes in October and November. If a stag came too close, you would light a match to frighten it. If it was not frightened or, more likely, if the match was wet, you still had three chances. As it knocked you down, you thrust the paraffinny rag at its nose; it would dislike the smell, and desist. If it continued to molest, perhaps by then another match would light and you could set fire to the paraffinny rag, with consequent terror and fleeing on the part of the stag. If all that failed, you could cast the pepper at his eyes or sensitive muzzle as he bent over to gore you.

This thoughtful procedure had happily never yet been put into practice.

'But they're dangerous beasts,' averred Geordie.

'No safe at all,' agreed Wull.

Both perspired freely, perhaps not only with exertion. Maybe this explained their desire for company.

We — though never hitherto driven to such precautions — were less inclined to demur in that thick mist, heavy with hoofbeats and reverberations. Meall nan Adharc was obviously a favourite spot for rounding up one's hinds and protecting them from enterprising neighbours. We remembered tales of unpleasant accidents to trespassing primates, and drew closer to each other as we plowtered on.

Then it all happened at once.

The bog levelled off into scree and the summit appeared through cloud a few yards ahead: boulders and two central quite rocky pinnaclets some ten feet high — a fascinatingly unsuspected tour de force from the landscape, which retreated on all sides pleased with what it had done. Geordie and Wull beamed at us. 'You see, horns — *rocks*!' said Geordie. 'Rocks — *horns*!', said Wull.

An appalling roar drowned everything else, and a great black-throated red-eyed bellowing stag leapt into view, with dozens of other dark shapes cavorting around in the mist. Antlers flashed and tossed; roar after earsplitting roar . . .

And, exactly as when we met the cave bear under Beinn a' Ghrunnda, we panicked; or, more respectably, our ancient reflexes belted us out of danger.

When I recovered my current self I was on top of a sizeable boulder; the Apprentice and the Doctor on tops of neighbouring boulders — and Geordie and Wull out of sight. We anxiously searched the ground beneath the beating hooves. No sign. Then a quavering hail from above, repeated more faintly still. Geordie was straddling one summit pinnacle, Wull the other. Their rucksacks and safety measures lay scattered below.

But we were not finished with the stag. A monstrous brute, a Royal if ever, it stamped and blew and trotted, bucked and swore and re-offered challenge. It was piqued by our refusal either to accept or to retire decently backwards, with our antlers lowered submissively.   It raced round and round our boulders, twenty peat-bedabbled stone of fury, nearer every circuit. It could — brow, brez and trez — sweep any of us off, especially the Doctor, whose boulder was a mere aspiring stone. Foam flew through the air. The Apprentice and I replied with pebbles, ineffectually. It concentrated on our companion.

'Shoo, blast you!', he shouted, and waved his arms.

Irritation increased. A maddened roaring, right up to him. He kicked at its snout. It withdrew, growling. Then it began to work up for a final attack, twisting and writhing, rolling eyes to heaven as witness, mobilising all its androgens. Hinds gathered about, adoring. It could not afford to make a fool of itself, this time. Dozens of sardonic young staggies were lurking nearby, to enrol disillusioned females.

The Doctor remained calm, hat jammed down. His eyes took in the distance between his tiny perch and the safe summit rocks. Too far, surely. To steady himself he groped in his pockets and began to re-light his pipe.

The stag was fully inflated for its final, pre-charging, roar, drones erect, when the match was struck. In the late afternoon mist and gloom the flare did all that Geordie and Wull had prophesied. The stag, too astounded to deflate, shuffled backwards, swollen. The ladies tittered.

The Doctor, seizing the psychological moment, struck again, bounded from his rock, swept up large pieces of scree and flung them at his foe. He roared most effectively and brandished arms long and antlerlike, sputtering occasional fire. The Apprentice and I leapt from our posts and joined the charge, pelting furiously. The stag disappeared, still backwards, still pop-eyed, drones in disarray, and full of unemitted roar. The girls shrieked with laughter and danced away beside him; one or two lingered to gaze admiringly at the Doctor. Other roars broke in below, from anticipatory rivals. We heard him far away, drones rattling, regurgitating a feeble and largely-digested bellow.   He was finished.

We left his successors to it, and hurried to the central rocks. Geordie and Wull leant an arm from their respective pinnacles. The crux was a definite Easy.

'They're dangerous beasts,' said Geordie. Wull agreed. 'No safe at all. You canna *trust* them.'

'It's the time of year,' said Geordie. 'October, ken,' Wull pointed out.

'Now's when they're bad,' said Geordie. 'The rut, like,' explained his companion.

We got them down, complimenting their stiff-legged agility. Wull had to go up both, in case the lower turned out really to be the higher. 'You canna tell by just *looking* at them.' The Doctor helped him, though less effectively than the stag.

When we regained the Doctor's tent the rain had abated. But a small burn behind, grown out of its banks, had fully explored our site. Cursing, we waded to the entrance. A quantity of burn was within, and fell out through the opened zip. The tent itself was unharmed.

'Gey strong tent,' observed Geordie. 'Canna find them like that these days,' said Wull.

But they were kind souls and we slept that night in Wull's two tents while they slept in Geordie's van. Wull's spare clothes were plenty for the three of us. While our bags were drying over primuses, Geordie and Wull entertained us with comic songs: duets. Geordie, unlikely enough, produced a guitar from behind the driver's seat, and Wull had his (two) tin whistles.

We turned in well past midnight. As we crawled, pressure-

cooked, out of the van, Geordie leaned over in confidence
from the back doors.

'It's a right good name for the hill — eh?'

We tried to reassemble thoughts.

'Meall nan Adharc — hill o the *horns*?' He grinned and put
two fingers on each side of his forehead. He bent his head
and said 'Urrrgh'.

'Like a stag — see? Eh?' suggested Wull.

They clanged the doors shut. We heard them laughing long
into the small hours.   By morning the rain had stopped.

13

An Occasion

'Of course we should go,' said the Doctor, sternly. 'The least we can do. He's a Good Man, and has been kind to us.' The Apprentice and I groaned. The back bar of Daddy McKay's gleamed in sympathy. There seemed no way out. Our consciences shared the same rope: the Doctor couldn't go alone. But he frowned. He drank thoughtfully; a good fifty pence of Glen Bogle. 'It might even be an enjoyable occasion.' He was unconvincing. We stared into our glasses; Glen Bogle stared back.

The occasion was to be the Last Munro of old Zero. Old Zero, *alias* The Reverend Zoar McKinley McSigh, M.A., B.D., had been a friend of the Doctor's at college. 'He always was an elderly-looking youth,' the Doctor recalled. Twenty-five years later he resembled a grave and active septuagenarian. He was the respected minister of a Wee Free flock in Glasgow, a staunch teetotaller and tireless campaigner for the Light, a diligent visitor of the sick and uncared-for. Distressingly admirable. He made us fidget. 'Excellent fellow,' the Doctor would say; and reach for Glen Bogle or its equivalent. The Rev. McSigh had nevertheless one fleshly weakness. He climbed hills. As a student he had climbed Salisbury Crags; but he gave up such doubtful adherences on ordination. A long hill walk inspired a wider view, and he persuaded his congregation that no trespass was involved. Certainly his Saturday excesses brought them fine draughts of fire and resonance the following day, in both Gaelic and English.

The path is slippery, however, and the Devil had whispered 'Munros'. . . . There was no excuse. True, the first Compleater, No. 1, had been a minister, but the Rev. A. E. Robertson was not of the Evangelical Free Church; and therefore no fit person to emulate. As with lesser men, totals inflated the head of McSigh. Pride lifted him continually above 3000 feet; outlandish hills were followed. Little by little. Until Auld Hornie had sold him the lot, and the last one was coming up this Saturday. It was Càrn an t-Sagairt Mór. Would so auspicious a name avert retribution?

No. To ensure infernal success the Tempter took on the irrepressible and rotund form of A. J. Evergreen Smith, who had completed them all — Separate Mountains, Subsidiary Tops, Eminences Furth of Scotland and the whole litter of Corbetts, Donalds, Dochertys and Maxwells — a dozen times . . . Evergreen, a compulsive organiser, happened to organise the Boys' Brigade in McSigh's district and soon swept the straying minister into intemperate and brow-knitting enthusiasm: the ascent of his Last Munro should be a Real Occasion.

Not only would the youth organisations of all the kirks in McSigh's district take part, but even the more able-bodied of his own congregation. And also as many as possible of the previous Compleaters would be called out, each identified by the number of his or her position in the Official List of Munroists as published (shame-facedly) by the editor of the *Journal*. All would assemble at the summit, where the Rev. Zoar would exhort them before psalm-singing and descent. Exceptionally blameless, if somewhat Apocalyptic. And the Doctor and ourselves were especially asked to share his pleasure. How could we refuse? Glen Bogle gave no answer. It glumly retreated beneath our eyes.

Well, we were there. At the foot of Càrn an t-Sagairt Mór. As expected, mist and drizzle. Last Munros are usually, despite the weather, scenes of alcoholic mirth, often of excess. This occasion would be decorous. At first, no stimulating beverage was considered; but the diabolical inspirer of Evergreen

Smith persuaded minister and elders, in view of the cold and exertion, to allow a little weak medicinal wine for those frailer members of the congregation who might need it — no beer, and certainly nothing spirituous. After all, a sip of Bouvier or suchlike celebrated physical thankfulness on these occasions in the old days. He even persuaded, with the extensive nether forces at his disposal, McSigh to agree to savour a touch of weak, very weak, medicinal wine himself at the top. McSigh had never — not even as a divinity student — tasted alcohol; his Communion wine was non-alcoholic; this was indeed a victory for darkness. He had wrestled; but — the Last Munro: just once, just once; to do it *properly*.

The Doctor had no objection to wine on the hill; he toasted Alpine summits with aluminium and *vin-du-pays*. But that week a rich and thankful patient had given him a bottle of Lochaber No More, the finest and rarest of malt whiskies, 16 years old and 100° proof . . . The temptation to alleviate the strain of duty was too great; he brought it with him.

From the busy group round the cars and buses that morning, McSigh came over. As a special mark of friendship he presented us with a bottle of wine, wrapped in brown paper. 'Just like my own — of course I shall take only a sip — but I expect you fellows will nearly empty the bottle!' And almost a wink from that clear blue eye: then he swiftly returned to the black-coated huddle of elders.

We unwrapped the brown paper, and stared. 'Sister McVittie's Medicinal Wine. Extra Weak: Formulated Specially for Invalids and Similar Persons.' Sister McVittie, unexpectedly rubicund, eyed us firmly and therapeutically from the label. She pointed unflinchingly at the small print: *Guaranteed to contain less than 0.5% ethanol*. We unscrewed the bottle and sniffed. Ghastly. The Doctor hurried behind the car. He emptied the bottle, washed it thoroughly, and almost filled it with Lochaber No More. He put it in his rucksack for the hill. He did not wish to hurt his old friend.

We relaxed, and set off. As we left, crates of Sister McVittie were being unloaded and dispensed, each bottle wrapped in brown paper, to the many Invalids and Similar Persons of

McSigh's congregation; they stuffed them hurriedly away in pockets and bags.

It was no climb. Wet heather and grass, uphill. Visibility, a dozen yards. Interesting yards. Across them passed a succession of improbable figures. Not only the elders and congregation, puffing and mist-dripping, in gumboots, goloshes and steel-rimmed spectacles, clutching black plastic bags and wilting umbrellas; not only the pink and uniformed Youth carrying banners; but also more familiar figures in rock-torn attire, some already well-stimulated and each bearing his number as a Compleat Munroist; the Mark of the Beast, as arranged by Evergreen's Infernal Master. (Prudence compels the narrator to change the numbers here and To State Clearly That They *Are* Changed . . .) Several, as a token of respect requested by Evergreen, were repeating for McSigh's Last Ascent, the self-imposed conditions of their own Last Ascent. They paraded like sufferers out of Dante. Number 112 was carrying a set of pipes, No. 105 a folding stool, 87 and 101 drove golf balls before them; 125 was having trouble with his skis. Number 172 was in evening dress, No. 230 in nothing but a kilt and a false beard. Number 83, who had carried his fiancée up, a wee smasher, in his arms, now followed obediently her matronly shadow; No. 76 experienced similar difficulty with his baby, grown too large for the rucksack, who stalked gloomily beside him, six foot three and desirous of Hampden.

Halfway up we came across Sir Hector Macassar – No. 56, an old vintage – sprawling on a plastic Inverness cape. Unashamedly, he was enjoying his whisky. He offered us some. The Doctor slung off his sack and in turn proffered our disguised Lochaber No More (Sister McVittie continued to point, unmoved). Despite Sir Hector's indignant refusal, we poured it out, pressed it within olfactory range. Whiskers twitched. Eyes widened. Mouth opened. Savour. Gulp. Savour.

'Terrific stuff, man, terrific stuff . . . Where on earth . . .?' The Doctor signalled silence.

McSigh had appeared. Well ahead of his flock, only the

fittest of elders beside him. He came up to us. Sir Hector, also once a fellow-student, welcomed old Zero and offered him a drink.

'No, no. No. But —' and here McSigh glanced almost gaily at his elders, who smiled grimly and inspected the turf — 'at the top I mean to take a wee mouthful: of weak, very weak, medicinal wine.' And he produced his bottle. Macassar sat up, unwrapped it and held it at arm's length.

'It's real!' insisted the unbecomingly enthusiastic Zero.

'Disgraceful,' observed Macassar. His further remarks were lost in the arrival of others. Among them were those two inevitable old summit-scavengers, Geordie and Wull.

'Awfy wet day,' volunteered Geordie.

'Could dae wi the sun,' suggested Wull.

And of course Evergreen himself, leading battalions of the young, his bald head gleaming with drizzle and pleasure, his twelve cards twinkling. About him dangled also multicoloured buttons, symbols of the various groups of sub-Munros he had conquered and reconquered throughout the four and a half countries of the British Isles.

We extricated ourselves, put Lochaber No More back in the rucksack and steamed on. 'Keep it for the top,' advised the Doctor.

At the top, there was some delay. The battalions had to be mustered, the flock folded and stragglers accounted for. Number 76 had lost his baby, No. 112 his low G. But it was a gallant throng. Banners dripped determinedly.

An elbow nudged me, hard. It was Geordie, offering a can of Export. 'Aye, doon wi it,' urged Wull, holding two. We quaffed. The Doctor was about to open our supercharged Sister McVittie: but the ceremony had begun.

Cries for silence. Banners dipped. The Rev. Zoar McKinley McSigh was balanced on the cairn and about to address us.

'My friends, this is a Happy Occasion. We have taken a rest from our Everyday Toil, and are gathered here together in the Clear Upper Air . . .'

Geordie, beside me, nodded and wiped froth into his moustache; drizzle beaded his sweating brow. Zero then elaborated the parallels with the Spiritual Ascent — the steepness, the backslidings, the mists, the rewards of perseverance. We wondered how soon he would come to the wine. Quite soon.

'And now we have reached the top. This Earthly Top; that is yet, friends, also a Higher Top. And we shall celebrate that Higher Top shortly, with all our hearts. But before celebrating that Higher Top, let us pause, and celebrate this Earthly Top. In an earthly way: for have we not reached here, friends, by an Earthly Way?' Geordie nodded. Wull drank noisily behind him; too precipitate — steel spectacles turned and frowned.

'Let us celebrate this Earthly Top in an Earthly Way, in the customary manner, before we go on, before we celebrate our greater ascent. Let us drink a toast to the friendly earth and stones that have helped us up, so far, so very far — though not, friends, far enough.' Geordie clouted my ribs again — 'Man, he gies ye an awfy thirst, ken,' he whispered hoarsely, 'ditherin-datherin awa like yon.' But the Rev. Zoar signalled down to his elders. Furtive rustling of brown paper behind the cairn.

'Let us therefore drink a toast. Some may wish water, fine burn water, others the juice of fruits, others, others' — he hesitated — 'others may be forgiven, perhaps, a mouthful of weak, weak, medicinal wine, for such an occasion, for such an occasion. O, it is a weakness, a failing of the flesh, for the flesh is weak in climbing a mountain; it is like embrocation for the stiffness or plaster for the blisters, on a mountain . . . A weakness, a failing, but' — (he was clearly anxious to get on with the experiment) — 'in-human-sympathy-with-those-before-us-who-sought, amidst-all-difficulties-of-stress-and-storm, these-heights-of-our-earthly-kingdom, we-will-celebrate, each-in-his-own-way, our-vouchsafed-and-happy-arrival-here.'

He bent down and was handed a large cup(!) by a frozen-faced elder. It appeared remarkably full. It winked over the brim as he stood erect. He raised it to his lips. A hundred other cups, glasses, flasks and bottles of coke were raised also.

'To our Bonnie Caledonian Hills and our climb beyond them to greater and more blessed Heights . . .'

He downed it. All downed it. Very felicitous. We were

moved. The Apprentice ventured not a joke. We were all brought up in good kirk-fearing households. And old Zero was so excellent a man.

He was also a thirsty one. His mouthful drained his cup. He looked surprised. The wine — even under the resolute supervision of Sister McVittie — affected him severely. He was quite unused to alcohol. He coughed, sneezed, grew red and watery-eyed. He swayed, and was helped down. Great applause, rapturous from the like of Geordie and Wull and Macassar, dubiously tight-lipped from the umbrella'd and goloshed throng.

Buzz of conversation.   Then a psalm began.

Having no book, the Doctor hauled out our bottle. He unscrewed it and offered it to Geordie and Wull. They read the label, glanced at each other, and shook their heads. The Doctor winked and grinned broadly, poured some into a plastic glass and handed it to Geordie. Geordie tasted it, blinked, and handed it to Wull. Wull sipped it, twice, and handed it back.

'Good, eh?' asked the Doctor, pouring some out for us. 'Sixteen years old, 100° proof, *and* the best!'

'No bad,' said Geordie; 'but no like whisky, mind.'

'Ay, whisky'd be the thing,' agreed Wull. 'Gey cauld here the now.'

We stared uncomprehendingly at their lack of taste. The Doctor shrugged, and swigged his glass.

'Grooogh!' He spat it out.

'Wine; damned medicinal wine! Evergreen's damned medicinal wine!' We all spat in sympathy, upsetting the damp-leaved psalmists about us.

'Some swine's switched bottles!' choked the Doctor. But his rage, and the countering belligerence of our shocked and hitherto tuneful neighbours, were lost in a growing tumult.

The psalm had ended. The crowd pushed forward. The Rev. McSigh, clutching his cup, refilled and respilling, was endeavouring to climb his cairn. Two elders were trying to assist him, three to restrain him. On hands and knees he reached the top. He was excited and flushed. He perilously straightened and stood, swaying. Then he began to bellow.

It was a rousing sermon, graphically if unconventionally illustrated. More of Paisley than Chalmers. Much was in Gaelic.

McSigh was above and due west of us; it was a westerly wind. We sniffed . . .

'Lochaber No More, by the Devil!' hissed the Doctor. 'He's been drinking our bottle!'

I glimpsed Macassar a little way along, gold teeth filling his whiskers, cigar in hand, gazing happily. It had been him; while we were distracted by Geordie and Wull and Evergreen . . .

A rousing sermon; but the preacher was profoundly drunk. One hundred proof, 16 years old . . . We listened and watched admiringly. He maintained precarious balance, on both cairn and theology. The congregation stood enthralled. Never had flames roared brighter. Calvin stoked furiously. Knox brought more faggots. Heavens! Another gulp from the cup . . .

The Doctor was about to scramble up and snatch it, risking unseemly altercation; when further fruits of error, rewards of Satan, tumbled to earth. A body of police, waterproofed, radio'd and ominously bulging, pushed amongst us.

The Inspector — our old friend McHaig — seized the Doctor. 'Ah, thank heaven, it's yourself, Doctor: what *is* going on here, now?'

A very puzzled man. We explained. He stopped breathing. Then he stepped back, slapped his thigh and began to curse, most frightfully and unsuitably. Our black-coated neighbours, breathless in their turn, white with horror, turned and engulfed him. One furious lady shook him, another slapped off his cap, another hit him quite hard with her umbrella.

Violence breeds violence. His men breathed deeply, felt under their raincoats, bayed, and likewise surged forward, grabbing most ungently. A regular brawl developed. We saw the helpless Evergreen, betrayed by the False One, delivered to judgement; his glittering badges proclaimed him ringleader. The Inspector ran about trying to call off his keepers of the peace. Scuffles, cries. We began to imagine a CS edge to the

westerly drifts of Lochaber No More. Above us, the sermon
continued, a uniformed interrupter being disposed of by an
accurate kick.

Eventually the Inspector, with the Apprentice's rather too
eager help, drove his men out of the fray. Order was more or
less restored. Silence fell.

We all looked up. The cairn was bare. No preacher.

He was lying flat beside it. Two elders lay beside him. Up-
roar again. Hysterics. The Doctor hurried forward. He knelt
by the victims, undid collars, felt pulses, listened to chests.

We saw, with relief, the bodies stir, and sit up. They rubbed
eyes and groaned. Two fell back and began to snore. The
Rev. McSigh, a man of steel, accepted a hand and was helped
up. The Doctor, ever sagacious, leapt on the cairn. He called
for silence. He explained that Excitement, due to the unfortunate error of our gallant police — who were looking for
. . . for burglars (unlikely, we thought) -- that Excitement
had caused Mr McSigh to lose his balance. The fall had stunned
him. But no injury whatever; perfectly fit. Though naturally
he might be somewhat giddy for a while, with a headache and
perhaps difficulty in communication for an hour or two. And
the elders? Ah, the elders had also suffered from Excitement,
but they were older men, and might take a little longer to
regain their feet; but nothing serious, nothing at all. Plenty of
willing hands. Let us continue with the service. Not spoil so
happy an occasion. Another psalm. Eighty-four? To *Martyr-
dom*? Let our good friends the police join in . . .

Cheers, clapping. Singing. The Doctor rejoined us through
an accolade of black gloves.

'Tight as owls,' he said, 'all three of 'em. The elders sooked
the bottle behind his back. Old devils. Hardly any left. Let's
go and finish it.'

A hand tapped the Doctor's shoulder. Inspector McHaig.
Sad and embarrassed. He drank the proffered glass without
a word. Then, nervously, he explained why he had been
summoned.

'A damned old fool' — a Major Pigstrap (the name sounded
like that, but surely could not be) — had rung him up ex-

citedly. Pigstrap lived just outside Balqueenie and had been taking exercise from his car, near the track up the glen. He had seen strange motor cars, vans and buses arrive. From Glasgow. *Glasgow!* Nosey-like, he had investigated further, with dog and walking stick, and had seen troops of people, some with curious bags, some with badges and numbers pinned on them; some in paramilitary uniform and carrying banners. All disappearing up into the mist. Some secret rendezvous. Many young, many older — old enough to know better, obviously there to lead them on, furtive, desperate-looking dark-clad buttoned-up people, grim-faced, determined — Real Reds they must be, Fanatics. And they were carrying, and trying to hide from him, brown paper parcels that looked like bottles — inflammable liquid? Petrol bombs! That's what they would be! *Petrol bombs!* And he had heard bagpipes — *Nationalists* there as well. He had asked a youth what was going on: the answer was sinister — 'A special occasion. Arranged for No. 293. *The Big Event.*' Secret, you see. Code. Cells. Pigstrap had crescendo'd by describing it, through foam, as an armed meeting of activist extremists who would afterwards descend on the, on the . . . McHaig looked grave. 'You ken WHO's staying there the now . . .'

The Inspector wiped his brow in anguish. It had *seemed* so genuine. Why, as they had puffed up — too misty for helicopters — they even heard singing. Impassioned singing. The SAS man attached to them (McHaig peered anxiously around) had unhesitatingly identified Old Hundredth as the Internationale . . . 'Ye cannae blame the lads, like . . .'

Nothing would happen, we reassured him. Errors were too evenly distributed. He came down the hill with us, his men limping behind. He ignored the ribald staggerers to right and left. He ignored the obviously unsuitable would-be drivers singing on the road beneath. He ignored the piper on the bonnet, hugging his recovered low G. It was enough to have avoided arresting the Rev. Zoar McKinley McSigh, M.A., B.D., for being drunk and disorderly and/or inciting to riot and/or civil disobedience and/or armed insurrection on the summit of Càrn an t-Sagairt Mór at 13.15 hrs on the 11th October, nineeteen hundred and whatever . . . A narrow escape. He pressed both the Doctor's hands silently as he left. From high above came wafts of (devoutly-led) thanksgiving.

The Doctor let the clutch in, rather cautiously. In the back seat, the Apprentice and I passed between us the much-diminished but authentic bottle of Lochaber No More. We had left Sister McVittie behind in the ditch. We lay back, content.

The Doctor swerved skilfully round an errant sheep.

'Quite an occasion,' he said.

14

A Stiff Upper Lip

'It certainly could be an aid,' agreed the Doctor. We were discussing the Apprentice's most recent acquisition, a moustache, in the not displeased presence of the new owner. It had germinated in response to his latest girl friend's desire for more public evidence of virility. It was indeed robust, disguising his normally sardonic upper lip with coils of easy splendour. He had grown it remarkably quickly.

'Could be very adherent on steep ice: should steady you, cutting out of balance,' continued the Doctor. 'You could lick it, to freeze in front of you; then breathe it off again and move up.'

The Apprentice swore it was not in the least an artificial aid. 'Grows naturally. Shaving's artificial; that's an aid. A right hairy bearded guy could get stuck in Raven's: never get up, whiskers jamming one side then the other, freezing on as fast as he's breathing 'em off. Shaving's the real Aid.'

Parallel B was coming that weekend. But when we arrived there, a violent freezing wind and snow squalls sent us up Raeburn's instead. The girl friend was Munroing nearby and we would all meet that night in the Inverfyvie Arms.

Raeburn's Gully is reasonable on a foul day and the Apprentice stormed it bravely, moustache as spinnaker. I gathered metal at the blunt end. The Doctor makes an excellent second on such middling routes, being tall, thin, and multi-jointed, and his long, prodding axe and nimble tricounis ran many messages.

Halfway up, just on the steep ice, came a prolonged halt. I peered through drift. My companions were crouched together on a minute stance, examining something inside the Doctor's anorak. Hell of a time. I shouted. No reply. I tugged. A tug back. Then the Doctor's eager beckoning. They had found something interesting.

Too interesting to take in the rope. I clambered up, cursing and coiling, points exploring powder snow. When I reached them, they were still in earnest conclave, the Apprentice fixedly eyeing his companion's bosom. The Doctor, looking down in a curiously strained position, explained.

A krab had jammed with ice. To thaw it the Apprentice had unzipped the Doctor's anorak and thrust the metal against his warm Shetland jersey. He had breathed on it to speed the process. Just then, both were drenched in a flurry of snow from above. Both had crouched farther, and the Doctor had instinctively zipped up his anorak . . . Muffled roars indicated that he had zipped it up into the Apprentice's moustache . . .

Painful trial had proved it jammed, not just frozen. Though, since then, tears and other secretions had welded the jam. The Apprentice was too sore to speak, and any attempt to move, let alone continue the climb as a joint lead, when so intimately and inconveniently mated, was clearly impossible. Yet they couldn't stay there. We had to think quickly, or permanently disfigure our leader.

As we had all forgotten to bring shaving things, I produced an ice-dagger. The Apprentice gurgled and clutched his companion appealingly. But I couldn't insert between whiskers and lip, and the zip was tough metal. So, to the Apprentice's howls and the Doctor's cries of horror ('. . . it's *quite* unobtainable now!') I sawed through expensive Grenfell and cut, tore out, the offending zip. It dangled free, and the Apprentice now bore a mandarin-like extension of moustachios. But he clutched his pegs with relief and straightened up, sobbing with drool.

The Doctor wrapped the ravaged garment about him and grinned at his leader. 'Looks just like that damn great catfish I caught on the Arkansas.   Marvellous beast.'

It was impossible to stow the two ends away without pain-fully restricting movement, so the zip dangled freely as the Apprentice raged up the rest of Raeburn's, fleeing from our merriment and roaring when, as often, an end jammed sud-denly in a crack. ('Try a tension . . . ' the Doctor would call up, unfeelingly.)

An hour later, he burst on to the plateau, through a goose-feather cornice. His moustachios now carried a fair weight of ice and snow and his appearance unnerved the two elderly climbers sheltering behind the cairn (we *had* to get to the cairn; the Doctor always insisted). We explained it was a special kind of moustache. (The Apprentice had signed us not to betray his shame; he was very sensitive by now.) They seemed to understand. 'It'll be a prob . . . prob . . . *feelers*, like? For finding the way? Like insects, like?' We nodded. They were relieved and offered us hot broth from a flask. We sipped gratefully. The Apprentice, however, went aside and proceeded to pour his share sideways onto his face. But the zip did not thaw; it was jammed. Instead, the broth froze; carrots and peas and things were added to his burden. He gesticulated at us as if imploring the kiss of life. But he was most repulsive, and only to be embraced by the desperately hungry.

It seemed he particularly 'desirrghed a drinnghk — cogghle?' We smiled, as at some defective, and patted him. 'Never mind; when we get down.' The Doctor, unusually, was whiskyless that day.

We roped down an easy chute. Descent was uneventful, though one tended to tread on the moustache at narrow places. Afterwards, an unhappy sojourn in a dense sitka wood. The Doctor, as always, encouraged the sufferer. 'Damned useful, in a place like this; how cats hunt at night. You know your own width exactly.'

At the edge of the wood we met a large party. The Apprentice being nearly all in, I approached them for tools — a hacksaw or nail scissors — for zip or whiskers respectively. Neither; they stared, wondering. Feeble groans of 'cogghle' again. Alcohol? Was that it?

The victim nodded vigorously, holding his ends, by now long, icicled, white and stiff. No wonder the others were startled. Their leader reluctantly opened his rucksack and, amid mild protests, handed over a well-furnished half-bottle of whisky. The Apprentice, to louder protests, scuttled off and, to violent protests, was seen pouring it over — not into — his face. Even the Doctor was irritated. 'That won't unjam the thing; it's a shocking waste — even of a blend.'

But the Apprentice continued to pour and began to tug at his adornment. He tugged and poured, tugged and poured until, by the end of the bottle — and to the stupefaction of everyone — he had tugged off all impediment: zip *and* whiskers . . .

'Good Lord,' exclaimed the Doctor.

It was a fake. A false moustache. Beautifully made, expensive, cemented by an alcohol-soluble gum. That explained the speed of growth — and possibly the short-term romantic intentions of the owner.

Who had been punished enough. He returned, nursing his lip, promising whisky at Inverfyvie. The Doctor meanwhile wrenched out his zip; it seemed more injured than the moustache. He pressed the latter to his own lip. Wonderful sight — a moose among seaweed. It fell off. We cheered. He rubbed it in some resin on a sitka trunk and pressed it hard once more. It stuck. It preened itself, if a bit squint and somewhat de-feathered. As the late bearer refused even to look at it again, the Doctor wore it proudly all the way back to the car.

We entered the Inverfyvie Arms. Noise, lights. Then silence. All eyes on us. Eyes especially from some posh persons in tweeds and from a jazzy-looking wee smasher. The Doctor met the gaze of the next-of-kin of a wealthy patient he had just recommended for psychiatric treatment: and remembered he was wearing a squint moustache. The Apprentice met the gaze of his girl friend: and remembered he was not. Panic seized both. Both leapt at the misplaced appendage . . .

Next Thursday at Daddy McKay's, they drank much and spoke little. Each fingered thoughtfully a small pink and white memento of surgical plaster.

15

Man's Faithful Friend

'Barking,' said the Doctor. 'Must be a dog.' We agreed.

We were engaged in a delicate traverse on Cir Mhòr; unfamiliar ground, but we had long looked forward to this week in Arran. We hoped for a good haul of routes, classical and spontaneous.

'Still barking,' said the Doctor. The pitch of canine communication reached a fresh urgency. 'Howling: blasted thing must be stuck somewhere.'

We scrutinised the crag above and below us. No sign. Yowl; yowl.

Five minutes later we passed a fierce rib (a triumph for the Apprentice, who took us round on a tight rope) and entered an echoing cacophony of distress.

'Down there — on the ledge below that slab. Poor brute. Could have been howling for days.'

We other two felt that the vigour of its summons indicated a healthy, recent and presumably uninjured beast, but followed down the Doctor's compassion, the Apprentice muttering rebelliously. A fine traverse ruined.

The Hippocratean oath did not specify dogs but, as the Doctor pointed out, there might well be a human casualty it was guarding. Greyfriars Bobby and all that.

But the dog was alone. It looked up at us appealingly as we descended the plump granite on small holds, the Apprentice keeping a good belay. 'It has the sense to lie still. Sagacious hound,' observed the Doctor. Its appearance was nondescript, a sort of Labrador collie, coffee and black and what could have passed, after a prolonged bath, for white. It lay quivering, tongue out, eyes rolling up at us.

'There, there, now, old chap, don't worry, we're coming for you,' cooed the Doctor soothingly as he slithered the last few metres.

His kennelside assurances turned to alarm as soon as he landed. For then the beast leapt up, barking and shrieking, slapping him all over like an ice cream cone with its tongue. It was a good five feet of fervid hairiness, and a difficult partner for so exiguous a slab.

'Get down, blast you, get down — Groogh!'

The Apprentice held us taut. 'Seems grateful,' he said.

The Doctor fought off the gratitude as best he could and sought to encircle the convulsive belly with a sling. 'He seems — geroff, poogh — he seems uninjur — foogh — uninjured; we'll have a job, though — hoogh — keep still, damn you, groogh — he's heavy.'

Gratitude, however, did not seem to include being roped up. The beast disengaged itself and retreated to the very end of the ledge, lay down, muzzle between paws, and whimpered, rolling eyes again.

'Come along, laddie, come along, then,' wheedled the Doctor, inching closer and wiggling his fingers persuasively. A rude gaffaw from the Apprentice above. 'He's panicky,' explained the Doctor, 'could throw himself off any minute. Poor creature.' He advanced slowly, whistling and beckoning, along a ten-inch ledge on eight hundred feet of rock towards a bunched and apprehensive dab of fur.

Then just before he reached it, the dab exploded, leapt up past him (he grabbed the rope, I grabbed the rope, the Apprentice leaned on his belay — miraculously we all stayed put) and with a horrible scrabbling of claws the animal writhed up a groove at the edge of the slab, up a longish rake, bounded over a crack, scrabbled some more and then stood above us on another ledge, looking down, feet apart, barking loudly and tail wagging furiously.

'Nothing the matter with the bloody brute,' bellowed the Apprentice, getting his breath back.

The Doctor was not so sure — some mental derangement — perhaps it had fallen on its head. 'No such luck,' grumbled the by now hostile Apprentice, dodging a shower of fragments loosened by the tail above.

Indeed, as we painfully clambered up towards its new ledge, the beast, joyfully exclaiming, leapt about upwards and downwards with astonishing freedom. To prove its point, it even revisited, briefly, its original ledge and marked it in conventional canine fashion. True, it slithered about a lot, and rolled over once, but was quite obviously at home. It needed nothing from us.

Bitterly, we resumed our traverse, having lost a good hour and a half. The remaining couple of hours were devoted to completing the route and cursing the dog. For it did need, apparently, company, and appreciated ours greatly. Barking above us, slavering (and worse), was the least of its demonstrations. After a tricky crossing of some wall you were met by a jumped-up fusillade of paws. If you grabbed it, it would clutch delightedly back and both of you would swing perilously over the abyss, held by your other two companions. Curses were instantly filled with (extremely dirty) hair. You would select the next foothold, step confidently towards it when, horrifyingly, a coffee and cream object would flash between you and the rock, brushing you off, and eagerly occupy the very place, slobbering down at you with pleasure as you sucked your knuckles and tried to clamber back. Kicking and beating were of little avail. They could not be too vigorous, for reasons of personal equilibrium, and the prods and punches we could give were accepted enthusiastically as part of the fun.

When we at length stepped on to the ridge, scree yielded more pointed argument; we beat the brute off, determinedly.

'I-say-I-say-I-SAY: what d'you think you're doing, eh?'

A string of disapproving tourists, wrapped in new cagoules and waterproof accents (it was of course raining by now), on their way back from the summit, stood and eyed us severely. The men were tight-lipped; the ladies murmured together. All fresh from Cruft's.

Too full for words, the Apprentice and I left the Doctor to explain, and trudged towards our next climb. He did not convince, and returned dejectedly, swearing beneath his breath. We heard bursts of barking along the ridge and cries of 'Heel, sir!'; and hoped.

But no. We were only halfway up our route when the damned creature appeared again. We were the preferred companions. It was a climbing dog.

This route was obviously too severe even for it, and it leapt about above, below, on all sides, yelping excitedly. It dislodged showers of stones, some quite large.

'Keep that bloody tyke under control,' roared a helmeted Glaswegian voice from below. 'You should all be on a ——— lead,' confirmed another. Further comment was extinguished by a basinful of gravel sent obligingly in their direction by our companion. We made haste. I saw a disapproving member of the Club on a nearby line.

And then there was an even louder noise from above. The all-too-familiar barkings were interspersed with shriller yappings, and then with feminine (human) screams. We groaned. A dog fight.

The racket increased as we neared the top. The Apprentice was greeted there by the boisterous hound and three shrieking women, clutching each other's windproofs. The altercation deepened with the Apprentice's own angry baying, so we hastened up, the Doctor, our diplomat, leading through.

'O — your — dog — your — horrid — horrid — dog has chased poor Manfred over the edge. O he is killed — listen to him, listen to him . . . '

The dead animal was yapping nonstop below us. It was a miniature pug, or some such affair, on a miniature ledge. It had obviously been led there by our — NO, not *our* — *the* great gangling brute, and couldn't get up. Its leader danced about, roaring advice.

The Doctor gave up trying to make himself heard, patted the least unattractive lady on the arm for comfort, nearly got assaulted by all three, and fled down to the puglet's ledge. He was still roped and a spare coil flicked the creature a few feet further below. Renewed and intolerable squealing from the trio.

'Shurrup!' bellowed the Apprentice, somewhat rudely. Open-mouthed silence. He felt he had to add something: 'Let the man concentrate . . . '

The man concentrated, on picking the furious Manfred up with least damage to himself. Carrying it was impossible — it wriggled, spat and snapped continually. So — to bubbling terror from above — he bottled it, probably upside down, in his rucksack. He knotted the loops with satisfaction. Then he climbed back up, undid the loops and offered Manfred to the bosoms of his family.

'O, O he's fainted, there, there, there — ow! — poor, poor Manfred — ow! — he's so shocked!'

We were pleased to see that Manfred's irritations included his owners. He bit unhesitatingly. A most unpleasant little beast. Fortunately they managed to fix a lead on him or he would have been off again with his companion, who sat regarding the scene benignly. He was dragged away protesting, chewing his lead with rage.

Animosity was general. 'Would you believe it, not a word of thanks . . . ' 'They all deserve each other.' '*Fancy* letting a dog like that run about on a place like this!!' Etc.

We had had enough, and turned down to the glen. We were too dispirited to kick, and throwing more stones was pointless. Whether they hit him or not — he was extremely agile — he brought them all back in triumph and ran off backwards, shouting for more. We had looked forward to food on the way down, but our pieces were in the Doctor's rucksack, and his oaths, unseemly for one of his clinical experience, gave us to understand that Manfred's excitement whilst confined had been intense. We washed the outraged equipment in a burn. Rather than let the hound enjoy our pieces we flung them into a deep pool. But he was looking and, leaping in, devoured them paper and all before they touched bottom, emerged grinning, and shook himself all about us at intervals for the next hundred feet or so of descent.

Our tent was fortunately fairly high up on the hill, away

from any of the day's human contacts. The dog squatted, damp and odoriferous, outside it. It had tried to enter several times, but was beaten back; its claws had been difficult to disentangle from the flysheet, and its smell still remained. We did not feed it (any more), but it did well enough off the Doctor's mince, put — for a fatal forgetful halfminute — outside to cool, and a slab of mint cake left in the Apprentice's rucksack. Everything, bar the dog, had to come in, and we spent the night cramped and apprehensive. Circumambulant sniffing and probing, punctuated by ominous and probably three-legged silences, plagued us and drove the Doctor, the unfortunate owner of the tent, to despair. Once he undid the door, shoved out his boot and struck a snuffling object. It was a sheep. But he woke the dog.

The next day we decided to traverse Arran, if necessary, to escape. We packed up everything and staggered under the weight towards the N.E. face. Our companion trotted behind, tail erect with well-fed affection.

At a signal, we stopped, abseiled down, traversed slab after slab, raced round the cliff, over the ridge, down, up and down again. We followed burns, splashing and tumbling with laden sacks, to shake off the scent. Up, and down again. Somewhere beyond Caisteal Abhail we paused. No sight or sound. We pitched camp, illegally, in some remote glen. We trembled and spoke in undertones. We encircled the tent with pepper, and slept with our food inside.

The next morning the sky was blue, the wind soft. Silence, glorious silence. The cliffs stood clear above, perfect. We climbed off, happy once more.

Then, as the Doctor froze. We heard it, too. Barking. Just up on the left, halfway among the slabs.

A terrible outburst of oaths was preparing, and the Apprentice had looked out a specially-sharpened piton, when we saw a line of climbers on the path below us. We waited and scrutinised them. They were ideal. Not VS men. Decent, washed, guidebook-clutching, mild-eyed. They doubtless fed blackbirds and cheered Royalty. They had pleasant innocent English voices and clean ropes.

The Doctor went over and explained. There seemed to be a poor dog trapped on the cliff over to the left. We would have liked to have rescued it but the way looked steep (we sat on our ropes and krabs) and his companions had injured themselves (our arms were stiff from hurling rocks): did they think *they* could . . . ?

Hook, line and sinker. They set off with a springy philanthropical step, thanking us for the opportunity, and marvelling amongst themselves at the probable agonies of the wretched, abandoned animal. 'Remember to feed it well,' called the Doctor. 'And see it safely off the hill . . . ' They waved, happily. They had a first-aid kit.

We did a small dance, and moved rapidly to the right.

16

One of the Least Frequented Parts of Scotland

It had been an interesting ridge, for that area of the West. We carried no rope apart from the Doctor's usual 5mm line, brought to assist any red-faced retrieval or, as the Apprentice suggested, in case we had to do up parcels on the way. We did not need it for either purpose, and enjoyed the day, wet as it was.

We came down on the seaward side. 'It's a pleasant route back; quite remote sea loch and glen. One of the least frequented parts of Scotland,' said the Doctor. Through the mist we glimpsed liquid confirmatory gleams. Also some sharply conical glints. These last resolved themselves into the turreted roofs of a Baronial edifice.

'Ha; Duntilty Castle,' remarked the Doctor, inspecting his map. 'And some shacks round it. Must have been done up recently.' Then clouds resumed.

Slopes levelled out. A track appeared, unsavourily trodden by man and beast. It led through a dyke. Leaping from slimy stone to stone, we became aware of a figure waiting on the grass beyond. Tall and thin in the mist, possibly potentially taller than the Doctor, but bent and wavering on the way. It was dressed in a kilt, a stick, a fawn raincoat and a Balmoral bonnet. It dripped. It eyed us askance, wavering more evidently; then, presumably reassured by the Doctor's tweeds — always our passport into the higher bourgeoisie of such regions — it straightened and approached. We stopped. 'Aah, hello.' A limp hand was extended. The Doctor, opportunist

as ever, took hold of it for the requisite second. 'Aah.
Howdyedo. Mkerrchkghnn.'

We stared. The accent was understandable; English Home
Counties, of uncertain reach. But that last word? It included
a much-practised guttural. Even our privileged companion
was at a loss. A repeat. '*Mkerrchkghnn* . . . ' Obviously we
were expected to reply suitably. Then the Doctor justified
his diagnostic reputation. The kilt, overlong like its owner
and stitched together equally close to the Thames, could have
been Henderson. The Doctor, well-versed in Telfer-Dunbar
and suchlike sociologists, noted also the moist Clan Badge on
the bonnet — MacEacheran? MacEacheran. A name. He
offered his own in return; these intimate canine preliminaries
concluded, conversation could begin. MacEacheran and the
Doctor stalked gravely on, avoiding the puddles. We, as
befitted our mucilaginous garments and the Apprentice's
increasingly far-Left expression, followed incognito.

Nevertheless, we gathered that Duntilty was now an Out-
door Centre. 'Toughening 'em up,' drifted, not unexpectedly,
from the mist ahead. At that moment, of course, They
appeared, from the mist on our right, a breathless and
stumbling downhill string of cagoules in all those fluorescent
hues most suitable for evening rush-hour traffic. They were
shepherded or, better, dogged — for he was tirelessly at their
heels rounding them up from declivities or growling them
back from watercourses they took for paths — by a short
square-faced man in an anorak as clarty as ours, and possessing
a sharp black Yorkshire bark. The convoy vanished ahead,
at a double-up. 'Rather reserved, you could say; but very
capable. Very capable.' Clearly MacEacheran preferred
someone else to administer the toughening process.

We reached Duntilty. The shacks were to feed and sleep
the wearers of the cagoules. They were spartan enough, and
moss already dripped from their asbestos. Our host, con-
tinuing his leisurely discourse, flung open the occasional
door: we smelt authentic wet socks and peat smoke. It was
cold and damp. Eyes peered furtively from within.

'Toughening, toughening. We make a *point* of Doing It The

Hard Way. All the three days they are here, they Really Go Through It. That's where we *score*. When our clients go home and say they have been to Duntilty, then they are *respected*. Their friends *know* they have Done Something Worth While, in these Too Easy Times. And, of course, Duntilty is' — he paused to enable us to take in the gleaming turrets, misty protuberances, invisible loch, wet gravel, and plastic St. Michael brogues — 'truly *Highland*. Scottish. Not like' — and he named a few of his good-clean-English-public-schoolboy competitors up and down the coast. 'Those places would be just the same in Cornwall or Wales or anywhere else in England.'

Not only Mountain Courses could be undergone by his clients. There were yet more expensive ways of getting wet. We saw ponies cropping the rushes; they raised mild and blameless eyes at us, and continued chewing. We saw dinghies, canoes. And all these courses were run by Dan, the anonymous sheepdog. 'He really likes doing it. Curious fellow. Doesn't seem to *bother* about money. Must say he's rather *valuable* — aah, ha. Now, you kind of people would be interested in this' — his uneasily seigneurial gaze included the Apprentice, who recoiled as from serpents — 'this Rock Climbing Boulder. Dan has fixed it up with all the latest gadgets. Like to try it out?' We demurred. A monstrous collection of cast-iron pitons and multicoloured ropes trussed up a glacial erratic beside the shore; it snarled helplessly behind them, awaiting the next Milankovitch cycle.

We also refused, politely, a not very pressing invitation to enter the Castle, where our host was installed and where his clients, after their gruelling three days, could recuperate, sampling Highland hospitality at an even higher exchange rate with sterling; but where doubtless the food and facilities, however dispensed, were an improvement on those in the sheds.

'Well, keep on down the *drive*. Then follow the road out through the *Park* — Glen Awley Park.' Glen Awley Park? The Doctor rapidly checked his map. On it, beyond that dot of Glentilty stretched, obediently, an unspotted Gleann a' Thuiltidh. 'Oh, the *map's* quite wrong. *We* call it Glen *Awley* now. *Anyone* can pronounce that.' Park? 'Yes, the Company's Executive Holiday Estate. Luxury homes you can buy, in a *quite* unspoilt setting. Swimming pools, saunas, air conditioning. And Sports Palaces. Everything essential to get away from it all. You seem to like this sort of country — have a look round. Mention my name. Sam Goldfeiner's the manager. Though I *know* they're all bought up years ahead. But we *are* building more, further down. Aa-ah . . .' And he withdrew.

Our subsequent conversation may be guessed. The Doctor soothed the Apprentice's Knoxian denunciations. He had visited workers' mountain camps on his Caucasian trip and agreed that in fact they were much better — 'Great fun if you like that sort of thing.' But he was principally amused by our late host. 'Marvellous Front-Man. Wonder what his real name is?'

So we traversed Glen Awley. Some of the white settlers' houses — the partly invisible ones — appeared reasonable enough; most of them resembled MacEacheran and his kilt. The glen, moreover, like the clients, had suffered Landscaping. The consultants' choice of Executive Vegetation perturbed the Doctor. '*Prunus serrulata* "Pink Perfection"': my God!' Still, a few natives had been reinstalled, at the back, respectful and peasant-like. Birch, for example; each one clean and firmly attached to an establishment pole. Behind them glared suckers from the *Betula* scrub uprooted to make room. The Lake — several boggy lochans commandeered into one — was redispersing to its constituent rushes, its willows beyond weeping. The tennis courts, however, introduced a pleasantly formal aquatic feature in this weather; beside it the copper-sulphate of the swimming pools appeared *arriviste*. We crossed a new but uncertain bridge and, except for the danger of drowning, could have knelt and kissed the honest hill-water thundering through; after three weeks of rain it sounded more like the cartographic Allt a' Thuiltidh than the Awley Burn its rustic notice indicated ('River Awley' must have been insufficiently Scotch). Yes, Glen Awley Park was plainly an Encampment, soon to join the other nettled patches on the hillside, a few of its Horticultural Society genes maybe ennobling the local flora.

Our sentimentalising was halted by the arrival of an expensive car, driven too fast for the road or its own motorway suspension. It slithered to a stop beside us. The driver was fat, pallid, bright blue-shirted. Obviously a Resident, presumably an Executive. The Apprentice examined his Class Enemy with interest. Residents had been hitherto invisible, no doubt at home scanning the oscilloscopic tartan of Highland television, or at the various Leisure Centres lightening their purses. The clouds of midges, attracted by such rich feeding, would have kept them in.

But this resident appeared worried, even anguished. 'Look, you're climbers. You can help. You must!'

The Doctor skilfully calmed him, and we got into the car out of midges and rain, now both heavy, while he explained.

Between mops of the brow and eyerolling through the drenching midge-beaten windows, he told us how his son, in the Fourth Form, a clever little chap, was up for the hols. A clever little chap, very unusual, fond of nature, archaeology and all that. He had left the previous night, with food and torch and all that, to climb that little hill — a shaking corpulent finger described an ellipse — to see how the rising sun shone through some old stones and all that. We glanced at each other: prehistoric astronomy again. 'You see, it has something to do with predicting times of the moon and tides and all that — to tell when it's safe to cross the' — he jabbed a more accurate finger towards the distantly-glittering Marina — 'to cross the kyle, in a coracle; and all that. So his book says. He took his book with him up the hill, O they shouldn't allow these hills, O he's such a clever little chap . . . ' The gifted youth had promised to be back by breakfast; he *had* to be back by lunch. And now it was after *tea* time . . . The hand-wringing gastronomic chronology indicated how gnawing the anxiety. Yes, he had contacted Mr Goldfeiner. Mr Goldfeiner had then contacted Duntilty, but Dan — who naturally ran the Mountain Rescue Course — was just now away again with clients taking the course and coaching them for the Pitfoulie Cup — for the best Vacation Volunteers. No! he had not left a note of their destination . . . Police? No, Mr Goldfeiner did not like troubling them yet — besides, he had heard three *climbers* were walking down the road.

The parent broke off, hands apart in supplication.

We patted him physically and psychologically and set off. We followed the boy's likeliest track from the house. We quartered the ground, calling and listening. Just as the sun was setting and the yellow security floodlights of Glen Awley Park were switching on, compound to compound, we thought we heard an answering shout. It re-answered, and we found him, down a hole between peat and boulders. The Doctor scrambled in; we stood respectfully by. He climbed out, cracking a joke, feebly responded to from below.

'Not bad. Coming down. Reading. Fell in. Broken ankle. Pott's. Clean enough. Need the usual.'

The Apprentice and I departed rapidly to the Castle, while the Doctor rejoined his patient, discussing the likely over-enthusiasm of Professor Thom. We found Dan and his team there. Also Mr MacEacheran, who was glad, because Mr Goldfeiner had *hoped* there'd be No Trouble. 'Most unfortunate for us if the Press got hold of it.' He phoned the parent. We heard, 'Aah — my dear Mr Chancy, happily I have found your boy safe and well . . .'

A Front Man indeed . . . When I steered the enraged Apprentice back to Dan, a crowd of refugees had emerged from the sheds; they seemed for the first time alive. They besought. Could they join us? I looked at Dan. He looked at me. He spat on the ground: Yorkshire for yes. We all set off, the Apprentice with Dan and his team, myself sheep-dogging the others, picking up dropped torches, separating gigglers, counting called-in heads every few minutes.

We met the rescue party coming down. The Doctor was galloping alongside the stretcher, still deep in equinoxes, the bearers well in the running for the Pitfoulie Cup. They left my excited gaggle far behind.

When I reached Duntilty, I found the Doctor laughing

heartily with a broad shiny individual beaming from disgraceful tweeds; surely Mr Goldfeiner? Even the Apprentice was grinning. All held large glasses. Mr Goldfeiner swept them aside, spilling precious millilitres, and thrust a paw at me.

'Great work, great work! Now everybody is fine and O.K. The ambulance is on its way, the statements have been taken, Mrs Chancy is happy and in tears, Mr Chancy is happy and in tears; and the boy is asleep.' (No wonder, after two hours of the Doctor on Alexander Thom.) He refused to listen to anything we said and bundled us off in his limousine, louder and plushier than even Mr Chancy's. As we left, we waved to the cheering clients. Dan raised lips from orange juice in acknowledgement. Mr MacEacheran, tired by the exertions of his rescue, had gone to bed.

I recall little of the rest. An enormous meal *chez* Goldfeiner, unlimited whisky (all, to the Doctor's well-concealed dismay, Dependable Blends of Staggering Expense), tales and stories (and information on Malts), songs in Cockney and Doctorial Gaelic, ballads on Brixton and Great John MacLean, a Yiddish aria by the ample Mrs Goldfeiner: and eventually blissful sleep in an executive suite of execrable taste, one for each of us. Then an early rise, an appallingly cheerful Mr Goldfeiner over a shuddery breakfast (we refused a further glass of Stockbroker's Pride), and a dawn whisk by himself, not his chauffeur, to our tents (and if ever we wanted a site and a *good* house, mind, a real *good* house, not their *usual* sort, and at a *sensible* price, mind, we were just to let him know . . .). Followed by a rush south to work.

We snored in the back of the Doctor's fusty old Mercedes, a wagon proper to our station. 'Astonishing thing,' the driver remarked as we boomed through a 6 a.m. Tyndrum, 'the number of people you can meet, in even one of the least frequented parts of Scotland.'

A fortnight later the Doctor received, with best wishes to us all, three cases of Glen Speerie, 80° proof, 18 years old, distillery bottled, smooth as milk; from Mr Chancy, a director of the firm. The accompanying letter added that he believed his grandmother had come from Scotland.

17

Blàs na Beurla

It had begun in Skye some years ago, when the Doctor, fresh from leading Collie's Route, had met an old man in the Sligachan bar who claimed to know the original name of Sgùrr Alasdair. 'No, no, it was nothing *like* Sgùrr Alasdair: that one is — an *invention.*' The Doctor, impatiently drumming his glass, had to listen through an hour and five drams of explanation concerning who invented the invention, and for whom it had been invented — all of which he knew already from a more accurate if less inspired account in the Club Guidebook. And so skilled had been the old man in the oral tradition that they parted without the Doctor having been told the Original Name. That might have been divulged the following night or, less improbably, *implied* several nights and bottles later; but the Doctor had been recalled to Edinburgh and an urgent case.

'You can only get these things if you have the language,' was his firm conclusion, based on that episode and on the proven extractive skill of his Gaelic-speaking friends at the University's School of Scottish Studies; their prowess was undeniable and often provided them with significant liquid contributions from us all in the back room of Daddy McKay's. The Apprentice and I, admirers of their bilingual persuasion, doubted if the Doctor, elutive enough in English, could coax even one drop, so to speak, of information in so athletically metaphorical a tongue as the Gaelic.

But he had worked away, building with grammars and tapes from our common foundation of the language laid in the

JMCS; hardly a foundation, rather an odd half-brick or two serving to distinguish (for us) a necessary mountain or a greeting from a farewell — but, when dropped accidentally and sonorously among native speakers, liable to engender uncomfortable silence. He did not involve us in his studies; we learnt, however, to interpret *'Tha mi sgith'* or *'Seadh, tha mi sgith'* or, more daringly, if emphatically, *'Seadh, is e mi-fhein a tha sgith'*, delivered, after some thought, in an off-hand manner following a hard day on the hill. Similarly *'Tha an t-acras orm'* signalled a slinging-off of rucksacks for a bite. We would reply encouragingly 'Buachaille Etive Mór!' or, more determinedly 'Stob Coire nam Beith . . .' We learnt also to live with, as with midges, his at first frequent outpourings (by torchlight in the tent) of Donnchaidh Bàn or the great Somhairle, versions which might have astonished the authors; but these books, too heavy or too expensive, gradually dropped from his climbing kit, and we believed the fire extinguished.

But Sròn Ulladale revived it. The westerly winds of Harris brought conflagration. Unsparing of our embarrassment as crass visitors from the *Gallteachd* and claiming proudly to host the linguistic genes of a native-speaking grandfather ('I'm only carrying it on' — or, rather, *'Chan eil mi ach a leantuinn ri mo dhualchais'*) he insisted on demanding food, drink, petrol or a night's camp site in the ancient tongue. Almost invariably, communication required restatement in lean unlovely English, due to insufficiencies in the Doctor or in the local inhabitants; one of whom remarked in unmistakably Lancastrian tones to his wife as we were leaving, 'That's the third Germans we've had this week.' The rare success spurred him out of all sense of proportion.

For we were most threatened on the climbs themselves. Sròn Ulladale at its mildest is, literally, still off-putting. We had gone there, after preliminary races over the sun-dappled Forest of Harris, to strengthen our characters, and for the Apprentice to liberate a few Artificials. Dangling in stirrups and harness, pulleyed to right and left, requires, as our unhappy experience on the Ben with *Constipation* demonstrated, swift unambiguous communication.

It was therefore just the place for the Doctor to announce that, as our progress in the language needed encouragement, he would speak for the rest of the holiday only in Gaelic. 'Even on the Climbs?' asked, with incredulous oaths, the Apprentice. *'Eodhoinn mar a tha sinn a' streap, a' bhalaich.'* (I shall rarely translate these italicised Doctorial utterances; the reader might as well appreciate how we ourselves felt at the time.) We did arrange mutual understanding of the terms for (or in the Doctor's mind approximating to) 'tight', 'slack', 'take in', 'ready', 'coming on', 'right', 'left', 'up', 'down' and so on. Even 'I'm coming off' was put into the tongue of the Garden of Eden, as befitting the preface to an imminent Fall. Mercifully, the Doctor was not (yet) familiar with the dialect of St Kilda, or we should have had further subtleties concerning the state of reliability of the guano underfoot (it usually dropped clear, anyway, from the Sròn).

It says much for the well-proven determination of our companion that he stuck to his decision, even when the choice lay between adherence to it or to Sròn Ulladale. His ribs became very sore. (*'Tha m' asnaichinn gle ghoirt. Tha.'*) The Apprentice suffered strain on his rope, his memory, his glottis and his temper, and fury drove him to spectacular successes, often virtually solo. He also took to going off alone towards the crag in the long evenings, while we lazed by the tents or fished. 'He's probably — aah — *'Is docha gu bheil e ag obair air* — aah — *rud ris nach eil duil againn,'** remarked the Doctor.

On our last day this surmise appeared correct. The Apprentice, strangely pleased with himself, led us to the most overhanging part of the great overhang. He announced he would lead it to the top, and then the Doctor would follow. Only the Doctor, for he couldn't risk *two* passengers. I felt somewhat nettled. *'Mi-fhein?'* asked the Doctor. 'You-*fhein*' confirmed our leader.

I sat on the heather and watched. A stupendous lead, marvellous to see. *'Schön, schön,'* cried the Doctor, gazing up, switched to the wrong waveband by admiration. *'Sgoinneal,*

*'He's probably working hard at — aah — a surprise for us' *Translator*

sgoinneal,' agreed a soft voice behind me.   I swung round and saw a highly attractive young woman, not a climber, and presumably a passing local.   The Doctor overheard.   He called out to her. '*Tha, gu dearbh, nach eil!*' She sniffed and moved away. It was clear what he had meant; I wondered what he had said . . .

He had no occasion to say more, for the noose tightened — 'Come on,' roared from above. '*Tha mi tighinn*,' answered the Doctor, and began. He did not perform too badly. But he was no Apprentice, and went for short voyages in space, scrabbling unbeautifully. The Doctor is far from vain, but he is human and male, and this exhibition, following the consummate artistry of his leader and so exposed to the gaze of an otherwise pleasing young lady, must have proved abrasive in every sense. It might almost have been planned by some ill-wisher.

Finally, he stuck. How, was not clear. Maybe the Apprentice, so far above, had misunderstood. The Doctor dangled, gyrating. Clearly he could continue if his leader freed the left-hand rope a little way up. He roared hoarse instructions — manfully as ever, in Gaelic. The Apprentice did nothing. I thought I heard the fair one sniggering. I turned round again. She was, but so were half a dozen other people. Some had plastic cases slung over their shoulders. Heavens! Photographers? Journalists?   Film men?   Actresses?

My heart bled for the poor Doctor. I bellowed instructions, in full Sassunach, to the Apprentice. He remained silent, flicking the ropes occasionally to ensure continued Doctorial rotation. He could be a hard man, provoked long enough.

But the Doctor was equally hard, and even more provoked. He gave up shouting to his leader and directed instructions to his audience, for relayed transmission. His period of rotation was fairly constant, so that the resultant intermittent foghorn, rebounding from Sròn Ulladale's impassive walls, was indeed ludicrous. I hoped the audience were laughing at that, and not at the Doctor's syntax — which under the circumstances, if not *foghlumaichte*, was certainly *bho gaisge*.

At last this Mórag creature (that turned out to be her name), flinging back locks yellow enough to enchain the most experienced poet, let fly at the crag a torrent of Gaelic. It echoed sharp and beautiful among the rocks. Then silence. What did she expect? The Doctor, as he spun, spun open-mouthed, like a goldfish circumnavigating its globe.

She got what she, the madam, expected. An answer from the top of the climb. From the Apprentice, none other. A long, apparently authentic, peroration — *anns a' Ghaidhlig* . . . Full and orotund.

And then, communication having been achieved, he wound on the Doctor; it had seemed to require, not just Gaelic, but correct Gaelic. (Being humane, he let his companion scramble fairly unaided to the top; but being human, he stepped carefully away before the Doctor got there.)

The Doctor, however, acknowledged a victory when he saw one. How it had been planned was celebrated that night at Angus John's, the nearby house of a *seannachaidh* whose remarkable songs and stories the other members of the party were recording (they carried tape machines, not cameras). Those long evenings had not been devoted to Sròn Ulladale, but to Mórag. And they had hatched together a pleasing revenge on the stubbornly monoglot Doctor. We did not enquire if the Apprentice could interpret all that his *ban-sith bhoidheach* shouted up at him, nor all that he so convincingly replied; but it was clear that night that some understanding had been achieved.

I cannot comprehend how we caught the Ferry next day. For weeks after, the Doctor hummed and chanted Angus John's nephew's cathartic playing of *Is fhada mar seo a tha sinn*: other pibrochs lapsed into mathematics. I could not forget Morag's mother's singing of *Mo run geal dileas*, one of the greatest of the *orain móra*. And until the next weekend, when we tackled a tremendous new route on Garbh Bheinn, the Apprentice could not forget Mórag.

18

A Daughter of the Revolution

That Harris episode brings to mind our experience with another young lady, rather different from Mórag. It is too long to tell here, indeed it is not yet concluded; but how we first met her and her companion may be of interest.

It was a damp August Sunday afternoon at Craig-y-Barns. Dismal; and the Doctor does not like popular outcrops of polished severity. They remind him of humiliation on the Junior Climbing Wall at Meadowbank. 'Like the end game in chess. Pure mathematics. Just no scope for the imagination. Mistakes are your own stupidity. Can be most embarrassing.'

The only thing he enjoyed about Craig-y-Barns was the firing, in the eighteenth century by some Planting Duke or other, of tree seeds from a cannon to the most inaccessible buttresses, as part of a re-afforestation scheme. 'Long term provision for decent belays. Curious how time disinfects ethics. Quite proper to use the trunks now; only the seed was artificial.' So he moodily scanned the botanical fringe. We had just arrived on our way back from the north, and stood beneath the Upper Tier of Cave Crag, wondering wetly what to do — if anything. But the rock was fairly dry.

Towards us came a Glaswegian hard man, with two people in tow. He muttered briefly to the Apprentice, handed them over, and was gone.

We gathered they were two of the very top American climbers. The Apprentice had seen them at Joshua and appeared duly awed. One was a dark intense bony girl about the height of the Doctor's anorak pocket, who moved as if on over-tightened springs. The other, a vast shambling ape, grinning from earlet to earlet, pink to the blond shadow of his crewcut. He raised a paw. 'Hi.' Both were in abbreviated shirts and jeans, the lady's being torn off some ten inches above the knee; which, for one of her height, was a fair way up.

The Doctor found himself beaming down at her. She eyed him from a set hickory face, attractive but for its likeness to some Aztec god of prey. He introduced himself. She appeared unmoved, regarding him fixedly with black unblinking lizard eyes. Her lank midnight hair disappeared behind into a grimy headband.

'I'm Virginia Prusik.'

'Ah — .'

'No. NOT the knots. Before my time.'

She turned away. He endeavoured to regain her attention.

'Ah, Miss Prusik . . .'

'I'm NOT Miss Prusik'

Unhappily: 'Mrs Prusik?'

'I'm NOT Mrs Prusik.'

The Doctor orchestrated all his bedside skills to suggest she tell him what she was.

She raised flawless precision-ground teeth, grimly.

'I'm Ms Prusik.'

'Ah, yes. Ys . . .'

The giant oozed across. 'Call her what you like, pal. Virge, Gin, Ginney, Pru. That right, gal?' He playfully nipped her arm. No impression on smooth hickory.

The Doctor, still fiddling with his wavebands, then tried to describe a meeting with Layton Kor on some North-West Orient flight. Kor had remained asleep until landing. Equal lack of interest here. She turned back to the cliff, devouring it hungrily, nibbling the turf of well-bitten nails.

The huge paw circled above us again.

'I'm Sep.'

Much less complicated.

Sep and Virge had been in Europe all summer. They had

just come from Sweden (why Sweden?). They were in Scotland to . . . climb the Castle Rock at Edinburgh. Of all places . . .

'Castle Rock?'

'Sure . . .' That broad easy smile extinguished further interrogation, even doubt. They would climb Castle Rock. Sentries, rockets, radar, would melt before them.

'Got a guide?'

The lady was back. The Apprentice meekly proffered that not inexpensive publication.

'That Rat-Race?' Jerk of polished head.

That was Rat-Race. 140ft (42m), Extremely Severe, E4. She handed back the guide and minced towards the wall with a curious springing step, like a female spider sizing up its prey. Then she returned.

'I'll need a diagram for later.'

The Apprentice handed over the book, she opened it, tore out the diagram, and handed the rest back to the astounded Apprentice. Then, still piercing us with a fierce visionary gaze, she fumbled in the debatable region between short shirt and shorter shorts; hauled out a grubby purse on a string, stuffed the crumpled diagram into it, and pushed the whole thing down again.

'O.K. Fine.' She turned away.

But we had been fascinated by the momentary revelation of a long twisting red and black tattooed snake down her middle, one end up under the shirt and the other presumably finishing below at some metaphysically suitable site.

Sep loomed over us. A great grin.

'You seen Ginny's Nature Trail?'

We gulped facetious nothings and followed him to the cliff.

They climbed of course solo. No ropes or that jazz. We were prepared for this by now. Most people on the crag were not, and clutched Perthshire appreciatively. Virge or Ginny or whatever was halfway up more or less the line of that E4, moving like a lizard on a 5.12: stationary, plotting, then a flash to another position; waiting; then another flash up to

the left, to the right; and so on.   Her limbs, though, held her
bunched body well clear of the rock; they curved in below
like those of a spider.   During these momentary waits she
was slipping, often from all four press-ons, but slowly, and
just before the movement blossomed into a peel she trans-
formed its momentum into another upward leap, became
again a trembling bud, even higher above our heads.   Unreal
enough on The Titan or any suchlike desert pillar.   Here, in
a nose-dripping Caledonian drizzle, a *montage*.   But firmly
pinned. She would not fall. Only flesh and blood fell. She
vanished beyond an overhang.

We resumed respiration. From up on the left croaked a
fitting opinion: 'Weel done, Cutty Sark . . .'

'Ye-e-e-eah.'   Sep shuffled to the cliff, tapped it with a
shapeless finger, beamed a great smile, and began *his* climb.

The technique was quite different. He flowed, rippled, up
the rock; but not elegantly. Like a huge *Amoeba* or pink
bathmat, extending amiable wrinkling pseudopodia right
round his periphery, tirelessly examining, rejecting, accepting,
moving on, using the whole of his oceanic frame, inside of
limbs, belly, neck or where his neck occasionally revealed
itself in the ebb and flow of that roseate tide. When he
revolved his head to gaze happily down at us, the infinitesimal
bristles of his cropped poll added their friction.   He was
dead safe.   The very rock relaxed.

'That's not a route . . . ' faintly pointed out the Apprentice.

Sep apologised, and hoped he hadn't damaged anything.

The Doctor congratulated him on making a new route so
soon.

Sep included the whole Upper Tier in an ample gesture,
without affecting his adhesion in the least:

'Guess they're *all* noo. Ain't never *bin* here before . . .'

And continued his vertical amble. We felt somehow
refreshed, as if windows had been opened. He coincided at
one point with part of the spring of *Mousetrap*.

Two Dundee mice had taken the bait, both white. Sep
paused to offer advice, then generously wandered up a little
with the rope to thread an aid.

'Now: that's just dandy!' And undulated on. (The leader did not return to Craig-y-Barns; but developed into quite a good canoeist.)

So Sep also vanished from our ken.

We waited below, but they never came back. We could have given them a hitch to Edinburgh, too.   Why didn't the Apprentice and I, at least, climb after them?   Well . . . as the Doctor said: after listening to MacFadyen for one night, he put away his own pipes for a month.

We heard nothing for a long time. They never turned up at the Castle Rock, either. When we did hear, they were at the Calanque, more suitable than Craig-y-Barns.   Yet we were fated once more to meet with them. . . .   But that is a different tale and, as I said, not yet over.

19

Winter Homes for All

The subject of snow-caves and igloos confines the Doctor, the Apprentice and myself to a frigid, glass-staring and cold-sipping silence. The whole bar contracts. These dubious habitations may well succour the sudden exposee or the ritualistic masochist; but to us were havens of disaster. They were frankly dangerous. The only two we managed to build each sent us back through the daily press as 'Climbing Casualties', an indignity which the more vexatious of our colleagues are too fond of recounting. I say *we* managed to build, but that is just decency; the author of their construction, and of our downfall, was — as usual — the Doctor.

Apart from himself, we doubted the value of what the Apprentice scornfully termed 'fall-in shelters'; though we had suffered much clubroom experience of snowholing and igloo-rearing from the extensive slide shows of Sir Hector Macassar and, less loquaciously but more factually, from the grubby-fingered syllabuses of earnest purveyors of Winter Certificates. We had also spent the odd blasphemous night 'up there' in a mush of polythene baggery reminiscent of a deep freeze two days out on a power cut. But we had never done the thing properly. We had never climbed a hill for the sole purpose of indulging architecturally in the Polar Vernacular. Until the Doctor met a long-lost nephew. He was an Antarctic geologist, and kindled our companion's creative fire with robust tales of roasting ice-baked nights, poker played in shirt sleeves, at minus seventy outside.

The Doctor thereupon bought a snow shovel, a large and glorified aluminium trowel, which accompanied us everywhere that winter until a certain day. Tied to his sack, it clattered irritatingly up rock, jammed behind ice in Parallel B, and at nights visited everyone's sleeping bag in turn. He would never leave it outside. We protested in vain. As demonstrated on our Cave Meet, he loves such incongruous apparatus. He reproved us sternly.

'You should always keep a shovel *inside* an igloo; in case of collapse.'

We pointed out that we were in a tent.

'Ah, well, in winter, heavy snow overnight: can't rely on terylene . . . Anyway, a damned useful thing to have around, a shovel. And this one fits in anywhere.'

We bore out his last sentence, groaning and prising the implement from between our shoulder-blades. But we had dissuaded him from purchasing a snow saw, presumably even better equipped as an aggressor, and considered ourselves relatively fortunate. The fad would surely pass. It was, so far, a bad snow year.

One February weekend we were bound for the Coe, but drifts blocked Glen Ogle. We left the car at a dripping farm-house low down and planned a round of Stobinian, Ben More and Cruach Ardrain, staying a night on the hill. We carried the Apprentice's new mountain tent that would sleep two at a clinch, and the Doctor brandished his shovel. 'An excellent opportunity!'

It was not. The strong wind blew the hills clear. Nothing but icy scree of the irascible and malevolent Stobinian variety. The Doctor poked and scrabbled below the unforgiving cliff-lets of Ben More late that afternoon, like an old yowe scraping for pasture. But only flour and marble, a few inches deep. No nourishment for his hopes.

Darkness fell as we clambered down the last rugosities of the steep north side. We were not very sure of our where-abouts. Bivouacking makes one cavalier of general topo-graphy. Our interests ferreted local cubic yards. We found ourselves below most of the wind, and the snow under the rocks looked flat; and proved deep. A similar scarp reared up beyond. A good site for a tent, even for a snow cave.

Indeed, excellent. The Doctor, uncharacteristically and execrably, began to sing as he wielded, at last, the glittering instrument. Blinded by his effluvia, we were forced to help and, despite ourselves, enjoyed excavating a roomy chamber in that huge soft drift bridging the trench between the lines of cliff. Although rock was a long way down, and flat, the Doctor dislodged a piece of quartzite after a deep lunge — 'Remarkably symmetrical crystal. Rarity. Museum might like it.' We dug midway in the trench, away from possible stonefall at either end. Scale was deceptive in that poor visibility: a Sudwand could be rising before us. The Doctor busied himself with ventilation. We, under continual instruction, modelled cooking shelf and sleeping benches. An ideal home, compared with the entropy outside and — for this once anyway — better than struggling with half-rigged nylon and string; mountain tents in particular seem designed on the windsock principle.

Supper was soon roaring inside. The Apprentice twiddled primuses, and the Doctor, to demonstrate the indubitable heat and to dry his breeks, lay stretched in sark, pipe and long johns on a luxury of plastic foam and eiderdown. Poker appeared imminent. Before joining them, I retired to a call of nature, cursing the wind and snow.

Returning, I noticed a glow to our east. The moon.

The moon? Rising very quickly. Surely, too quickly . . .

Showers and gobbets of snow streamed up through the illumination, heavier each minute; billowing hypnotically.

I struggled along the trench towards this odd phenomenon. Then the moon rose.

Two moons! Two huge eyes of light, centres of roaring snowy Catherine wheels. And a smaller yellow intermittent light above them. Twinkle, twankle, twinkle . . .

Somehow strangely familiar . . .

With horror, I guessed the unguessable. A snow plough!

Snow plough!

On Ben More . . .

Topographical niceties aside, it had to be stopped; or our housewarming right in its track would be rotovated, my companions likewise.

I staggered in front, and danced about.

It continued, bellowing and gnashing, sooking up the stew.

I leapt at the choking bank, nearly slithered into its threshing maw and booted chains; I beat the heartless yellow flanks.

It kept on, masticating furiously, head down.

Only twenty yards, at most. I bashed the side window so hard it nearly split. The brute felt that. It reluctantly slowed; and stopped, panting and grinding with impatience. I nursed my numbed wrist. The window screwed down. A wool-encumbered orangehooded scarlet head peered out.

'Ay, ay?'

I attempted to shout an explanation. The head, as ponderously deliberate as the rest of the vehicle, turned to another, unseen, head within. Then returned to me.

'Oo, aye; we'll get ye oot as soon as we can!'

Disappearance of head.

Fearsome revving and, Lord, the contraption began again. I clung to the lurching window and tried to convey an urgent necessity of stopping BEFORE they got my companions out.

Fifteen yards on, it did stop. My information had maybe penetrated the well protected epidermis of the Coonty roadmen, substantial enough in its own right; but probably more effective in instilling a sense of the unusual was the capering figure of the Doctor, aroused by the glare and thunder, bare feet and shirt-tails flapping, horrific in the stormshaken — but now mercifully stationary — headlights. The Apprentice, eyes popping and primus still in hand, filled in a confirmatory corner.

'What's all this; like?' Heavy consternation at the windscreen. Three heads.

We had stopped them; but explanation was impossible. They were too well wrapped in years of rescuing foolish but grateful motorists. And were they not this very night grinding up from Killin to liberate more of them stranded by Loch Dochartside? And were not their rivals from Strathyre,

Dalmally and Glen Falloch nosing at the same harvest, muzzles lowered, diesels wagging?

We gave up; and dragged, still shocked, our belongings out of the centre of the A85, stuffing everything — including a pan of hot fried bacon and two cupfuls of soup — into the nearest rucksack. The Doctor's museum specimen — most likely a reflector from the invisible white line — was not included. The roadmen had climbed down stiffly, and stood in a group, hood-scratching, bemused at finding no car, but a Hole . . . like. While the Doctor once more endeavoured to explain, pulling up his breeches, the scene changed dramatically. *Blue* lights flashed. A police Land Rover, two Land Rovers, appeared. Torches.

Explanation was clear to them. Our open rucksacks, dishevelled attire . . . Lost climbers, distraught, about to collapse from exposure, gear scattered despairingly. Obvious. We were led away amid scribbling and earphones, protesting unavailingly against omnipotent sympathy. There were flashes, clicks: reporters occupied a third Land Rover . . .

The second occasion was still worse. Let me continue. It is good for the character.

Many weeks elapsed before the Doctor dared mention the subject again. He took us in fine vintage style (the leader *must* not slip!) up a spring-ice S. C. Gully, and we relented. On condition that whatever edifice, or declivity, he raised, or lowered, should be well away from danger of Public Instrusion. We wanted a quiet home of our own. Not too near a main road . . .

'Quite so, quite so. How about a summit plateau? Safe enough there, eh? Not the Gorms, of course: that's a helicopters' main road. Somewhere else . . . Splendid at this time of year. You can get good windpacked igloo snow; and lie at your own door drinking-in the sunset.'

We agreed because it sounded impracticable. Wind would remove snow, not pack it, from so exposed a position. Alas, that very week in late April snow fell heavily high up without a wind, and was then compacted by tiresome zephyrs. So the following Saturday found us on the top of Meall Chuaich — remote enough — in cold sunlight, being supervised in fetching and carrying, and even in cutting and shaping, blocks for an igloo. A Thick-walled Igloo, best for Scotland.

The Great Pyramid had scarcely required more expertise. Mutterings and hummings. Angles and tapers. Punctuated by a long description of anchorites' cells on some Irish island. 'Not a trace of earth or mortar. Drystone beehives. Much more difficult than an igloo. And devotions five times a day as well. Devil of a job . . . ' But we enjoyed silkily carving the sighing whiteness, so light and firm; pressing the blocks to mutual embrace; subtly aligning blue joints of shadow.

It was a beautiful object when completed. On the white dome beneath cloudless azure, it glistened irreproachably. The grimy summit cairn, its nearest rival, was half-buried a good three feet lower.

The Doctor patted it continually, unable to resist paring here and encouraging there. 'You know, it's almost a Thin-walled Type. A perfect hemisphere up top. Pity we didn't have that snow saw: would have been much quicker.' We shuddered; we had tripped over the shovel several times already and anticipated another night of its pressing attentions. Yet it had performed well. Ample room for three or four, even for itself; an ice age howff, with almost full headroom and built-in kitchen and bunks. A tunnel led up from the entrance, to drain cold air. A primus polished the interior finish of Glacier Blue to non-drip gloss.

We duly lay outside a little in the Doctor's sunset, cooling off, watching the round miles of snow about us redden and purple, above the dark glens of Laggan. Then, a flaring feast inside, the décor now Primus Orange. We relaxed on foam and feathers. A tiring day. But the Doctor insisted on poker; just to demonstrate.

A comfortable night. No damned snowploughs. Dispensing with adiabatic aids, we corked the tunnel with a rucksack to deter inquisitive summit winds. Snug, we trusted the ventilation holes. Jerseys, breeks were discarded. We were very warm. The Doctor purred. 'Even at seventy below . . .'

Carbon dioxide is soporific, poker (with the Doctor) exhausting. I remembered nothing. No dreams. Not even a shovel. We snored long, disgracefully long, into the Sunday morning.

The Sunday morning was clear and fresh, and under its genial spring sun the high eastern plateaus gleamed and sparkled. Ptarmigan chattered, skiers queued, and up to the welcoming heights wound a bright and early crowd of Young People, shepherded by the eternally ebullient A. J. Evergreen Smith; eager for their first real Munro. They stomped on to the plateau and streamed towards the distant cairn, hullooed by the perspiring Smith. Evergreen's dog, a large exceptionally brainless redhaired creature, Doggie by name, barked in encouraging circles. They reached their cairn, their dream, and danced round it in snow already trampled by previous triumphant Munroists. Doggie claimed it as his own several times. In great excitement, all twenty were successfully counted. Then there had to be the group photograph. As many as could, clambered up the cairn, Doggie as well. Evergreen teetered at the apex, dangling the two jumping smallest. The rest clustered about, buzzing and singing round their ample queen, swinging hands and kicking toeholds. They hurrooed and kicked and barked again and again as the camera was set up. They hurrooed and kicked and barked once too often.

They all fell through.

The whole clamjamfrey. Right through.

On top of us . . .

I was dreadfully wakened. Avalanches, earthquakes, stampeded through my brain. I glimpsed blocks of ice and daylight, boots, legs, hairy socks, a sort of tail: a haggis of snow, shouts, barks and screaming. An inexplicable, appalling chaos. I sank back, refusing to believe, buffetted and pounded . . .

They scrambled off, pulled each other out. They were counted again, all heads extricated and dusted free of snow. Twenty . . . Twenty . . . two. Twenty-two!

Evergreen, agape, counted once more. Who, how?

The Doctor and I found ourselves hauled to the front, through a forest of legs and a tail, I still halfawake, the Doctor hopelessly disoriented; and, unhappily, again in his underclothes. Young Folk shrank away. Silence reigned, even over Evergreen.

As I felt someone should say something, I opened my mouth; but found myself describing the second Pyramid. The Doctor, collecting his agitated neurones rather better, took over, though he did begin with a few words on the Great Skellig. He soothed them, had them (inevitably) cheering again. Someone hung a cagoule about his knees.

Then we remembered the Apprentice. Scattering brats, the Doctor and I plunged into the ruins. But Doggie had found him, probably had claimed him as his own, and was now affectionately slorping over his furious purple face. He was iced in, halfway down the cold air trench, and felt like it. He was fortunately gagged by a largely unbitten block and before removing it I drew his attention to the younger and more innocent of our visitors. He was, however, beyond swearing.   I prised the shovel from the small of his back.

Swearing began when he found he could not kick at the dog nor even rise without pain; and when the Doctor, now more professionally back in breeches, diagnosed a couple of cracked ribs: probably the shovel, but possibly the still-wondering thirteen globular stone of Evergreen. He refused to be strapped up, still less carried; and as he clearly could not walk down, a dilemma ensued. It was resolved by the presence of an attractive darkhaired student nurse, a slender but firm pillar of the Youth Group. He consented to be strapped by her, in decent privacy beyond the rubble; and accepted her unyielding arm on the long limp down.

Doggie galumphed about in front of the Casualty, cheering him on. Boots were restrained by painful ribs and Nurse's grip, but when the feckless animal bundled once too often against his legs, the Apprentice got in a good Penalty before collapsing. Howls (from the dog) brought Evergreen bounding across from a short tutorial on pollination in *Juncus squarrosus*: 'Ah, poor, poor Doggie, THEN . . .'   They clung together, the hound casting large white reproachful eyes back at an unrepentant Apprentice, now suffering Florence Nightingale's tongue. There is no malice in Evergreen. He twinkled at us brightly: 'Ah, yes, Doggie *can* be *very* troublesome.'

But Doggie won. Next day his picture was larger than ours. Heroic Doggie. Who smelt out an Injured Climber Buried Under The Snow. A complacent hound across the front page. Beneath that, a horizontal Apprentice; a third, much smaller, picture of the Doctor and I, merely rescued together. A long, graphic story. Doggie's master is a dab hand at the newspapers. But nothing about a collapsed cairn. No shred of malice in Evergreen.

The Doctor and I, gloomily predicting all this, hobbled down after the excited gaggle. Painfully the Doctor stopped, painfully felt behind, painfully slipped off his sack; and rummaged within. He looked up, stiffly.

'Blast. It's not here. Must still be under the snow.'

The shovel. The bloody shovel.

We called it a spade, and left it there.

KENNEL NOTE: We were of course too hard on poor Doggie; we felt savage that day. Doggie is a kindly beast, only a little less intelligent than the average M.P., and quite guileless; not like that vile Climbing Dog of Arran. We have frequently met him since, and fondled his long floppy ears. A thing we would not do to the Climbing Dog of Arran. Nor to the average M.P.

20

Old Man Ahoy

Even before this, I had not liked sea stacks. They were so crude and digital, mere exclamation marks against the solid statement of cliffs about them. And, looking down from their tops, one lurched slowly and flatulently to and fro on a smearing tide. But the Apprentice revelled in their verticality, and the Doctor elaborated on their character — 'you get to know them from every side,' he said.

They all had similar names — Maidens or Old Men — and this one was an Old Man, an Am Bodach, off the west coast; its precise location, for reasons obvious later, cannot be given. The Doctor had climbed some of its fellows with Patey, but they had never got round to this. It stood some way off a steep deserted shore, racked by savage tides. Approach needed planning, and several days.

That summer the Apprentice and I, after a week's climbing, were to be met by the Doctor at the coast not far from the Bodach. He was driving up with his new rubber boat and its powerful outboard. He was late, and when he did arrive he was a bitter man.

'Wrecked,' he said. How? we asked. 'That blasted beech!' he said. What beach? 'A huge brute, right over the road. Couldn't avoid it.' Our disturbing impression of some massive maritime incursion was soon corrected. The boat had travelled on the roofrack, the road was narrow, and a damned caravan ('those *damned* caravans!') had swung inexpertly at him; he swerved to the verge and ripped the port float end to end, on a bough of *Fagus sylvatica*. The deflated ruins draped the back seat. In the boot reposed the 10 h.p. Volvo outboard.

'We'll have to look for another boat to fix on the end of it,' was his conclusion. But no boat could we find. Nothing that dared to wear such internal combustion. The few houses along the coast were occupied by old women ('no, no: no boat') or holidaymakers (largely inflated ducks). The Doctor refused to enquire at the numerous caravans. Someone (a harmless Frenchman or southern Englishman — it was difficult to tell, his vowels were so confused by the Doctor's expression) suggested the Warden at the Nature Reserve. Still bad-tempered, the Doctor strode along to a No-Entry sign. We lifted the wire and walked on. A terrible smell (soon to be familiar): rotting seaweed, birds. Birds everywhere. Feathers in the air. Continual squawking. Not *still* breeding?

The warden was a mild man, Jim Twite, holding a revolting bald gosling-like individual in each hand. So guileless were his eyes that the Doctor did not like broaching the boat business right away. We therefore, as supposed bird lovers, underwent the story of how the Twites (his wife joined him, nursing two equally repellent, but smaller, neonatal *Anser anser*) had tired of living in Blackburn, and how rewarding they found it up here, re-establishing a colony — he indicated the clamouring throng that crammed the bright green fields of an evicted township — and combing innocent feathers free of oil. The Doctor thought of his engine, and hesitated again; allowing a further half-hour's conducted tour, family to odorous family, before he could lay the problem before our hosts. We needed to hire a boat for rough seas and for a 10 h.p. outboard. Mr Twite — Jim — placed his pair of offspring — orphaned from the egg — carefully on the heads of the other two held by his wife, wiped his hands clean on his jeans and said:

'I'm not sure that I can help you, we've not that sort of boat, it's only for calm weather, pottering-about-like, it wouldn't stand the strain and the noise would upset our birds, wouldn't-it-Edie, but — why don't you try the old man?'

We explained we indeed hoped to go to the Old Man: that was precisely why we needed a boat.

'O but you can easily walk to the old man, it's only a couple of miles up the path isn't-it-Edie?'

We said that the Old Man was out at sea — didn't he know?

'O he *has* been out at sea some time ago, and he still goes out a bit, but he's really more or less fixed on dry land now, isn't-he-Edie?' Jim flashed a smile, returned thinly by Edie. They peered at us intently.

This further suggestion of coastal mutability worried us. The Apprentice, scenting confusion, volunteered that our Old Man was known as the Bodach.

'So is Donnie, by the old people here,' said Mr Twite, 'they call him the Bodack.' He looked at the Doctor. '*Bodack*, they say, used to mean "old man". That's because he's an old man, you see.' Dawn broke.

Mr Twite, resuming his fostering of the pimply and objectionable pair, who were now calling loudly, stretching skinny winglets and performing other physiological functions, pointed the way to Donnie McIsaac's; he held a bemused infant at arm's length to the north-east. 'Up there,' he said.

'Eh, it was funny,' he went on, 'getting mixed up like that, wasn't-it-Edie. Now Donnie is a very old man, over 80 isn't-he-Edie, but he's very active and I know he has a lobster boat with an engine, too, he's a nice old man but can act strange, can't-he-Edie? But you *do* know, don't you, you're not allowed to *land* on that rock,' he added, 'it's bad for the birds.' 'There's an *order* on it,' hissed Edie, thrusting up her spectacles, 'but you *can* have a sail *round* it — it's very *in*teresting . . .'

The track passed more caravans, glassy packets of suburbia parked on the Precambrian. The inmates protected themselves, pot plants and small pet carnivorae from the blast of wind and landscape by plastic embattlements. We did not disturb their privacy. From one, to the Doctor's consternation, came the News in Gaelic.

As the track got worse, his temper improved, and when it had disappeared and a hut, presumably Donnie's, had come

in sight, he was the familiar Doctor again. He discussed plans
for hauling the outboard all this way. 'Perfectly possible.
With determination. Or a pony.'

But before we reached Donnie, a wire fence blocked our
progress. Twelve foot high, bristling with barbs and —
unpleasantly — with insulator-like things. A large red and
white notice announced, aggressively, 'Keep Out'; another,
still more aggressively, 'Ministry of Defence'.

We were probably near a N.A.T.O. frontier. We had noticed
English and American Army trucks back by the Nature
Reserve, and an emptiness of beer cans about the place. We
trod carefully, the Apprentice, a dedicated dissident, this
time indulging a rave.

Donnie's house was outside the fence. He had refused to
move, not desiring the generous financial reward offered on
behalf of Democracy. As the ultra-left-wing Oban Free Press
printed his picture several weeks running, he had to be allowed
to stay. The fence bent in, and then out again. It gave good
shelter for the tatties in an east wind.

Donnie himself understood at once; we could see Am
Bodach from his doorway, a kind of fractured Statue of
Liberty standing out from an iron band of cliff. We might,
yes we might, be able to drag the outboard here. But that
would be no help at all. Because he would not let us use it on
his boat. His boat had an engine of its own. What use would
another one be? Moreover, the stern was not *built* for an
outboard. Just look. Not *built* for an outboard. He gazed
placidly over his pipe at us. He was as tall as, as erect as, and
had been considerably broader than, the Doctor. It was
pleasant to lean on the dry-stone wall of his gaze, after the
uncertain journey hitherto. Only his right hand — not
unnaturally at eighty-three — shook a little as he shifted the
bowl of his pipe.

Would *he*, then, take us to the Bodach?

What would we be going there for? Would we be geologists,
hydrologists, ornithologists, ichthyologists, algologists, ecolo-
gists, divers after the sea urchins? He rolled the catalogue past
his pipe stem. He had suffered them all.

Because if we were — No. He would not hire himself or his boat.

Puff. A ghost of a hard smile.

The Doctor warmed to this excellent rock.

'We only want to try and climb it. Nothing else.'

'Climb it? And what is the use of that to anybody?'

'None whatever.'

It was the right tack. The Doctor can afford 10 h.p. Swedish outboards, even under the National Health Service, because of skills like that.

Puff.

If we only wished to visit Am Bodach for our own enjoyment, he would take us there. But he could not guarantee an easy landing, or a take-off on the same day. The swell.

No matter; we had bivvy bags, spare food. Am Bodach had been climbed?

'Who would want to climb it?'

The Army, we suggested.

His eyes fixed bayonets. No; not even the Navy.

It was expensive, but promised to be worth it. We lugged our gear to Donnie's, and camped on the foreshore. Behind some rocks, because The Army was always watching for people . . . We understood.

The next day was fine, but with the usual swell. We pushed out Donnie's boat and loaded her up. He swung aboard, poled out a little, then lifted wooden hatches. Still bending, he gazed skyward and turned and turned a handle. Eventually a splutter and clangorous rumbling. He replaced the hatches, took the shuddering tiller, adjusted his pipe, and steered us out of the bay.

It was a frightful coast. The base of the cliffs — two hundred feet high or more — heaved and seethed; foam broke and was swallowed, was vomited out again. All in silence. Nothing could be heard above the engine's din. We tried to plant a conversation on Donnie. It blew off. He puffed, unmoved.

There were terrifying incidents. Just out of the bay, where we met the swell (delivered straight — but for some irritation

about Lewis — from Labrador) and where the bow began to
rise and smack, smack, each shouldering monster and the
spray flew, just out of the bay and beside the great guarding incisors of basalt, the engine stopped. A rushing,
drenching silence. We were slung sideways at once. We had
only one oar. 'Hold her out,' said Donnie, resigning the tiller
to the Apprentice. He bent under the hatches. Minutes,
minutes. We kept her bows out, but were driven ever nearer
to that boom and suck and explosion at the root of the cliff.
He rose and held something in his hand. He lifted it up,
looked along it and blew. He inspected various other objects,
staggering as the boat staggered. Heavens — parts of the
engine! If he dropped one . . . He picked up an old bait can
from the scuppers. He leant over the side, swilled out its
molluscan residues in a passing wave, shook it, and poured
in petrol from a rusty container. He was washing the pieces
of engine. He took them out, examined them, blew, replaced his pipe and stepped back to the hatches. We had
only a dozen yards to go; the backwash from the cliffs
drenched the crouching Apprentice in the stern. We
wondered if any gear could be saved. The plunging and
thunder and rock promised little enough for ourselves.
Donnie inspected the sky from the hatches; he was turning
the handle. A sputter. A stop. A sputter, a stop, a jangling
roar, hatches back, he took the rudder, away we went.

'Dirt in the carburettor.' The message was passed hoarsely
each to each, as we clutched the gunwales.

It happened twice again, but seemed safer farther out.
Then the stack was above us, rising and falling.

'Because it is calm the day, we can get near enough,'
shouted Donnie. We were only six or so feet from a curling
slab that lifted and dropped almost that height as the swell
travelled along it. 'This is the landing place. Where we used to
come for the eggs. Take your rope and jump for it.'

The Doctor, anxious to board first, flung off his jacket,
gripped the coil, balanced on the prow and awaited the next
upward lunge of the slab. As it appeared, he jumped; but just
before he jumped, the engine sputtered again. We lost way,

and he plunged straight into deep water.

When he came up he ignored the boat and struck for the slab, was lifted over it by the swell and, jamming his fingers into crevices, clung to Am Bodach. He curled up legs, survived the next swell, and then clattered (he was in nails) up a barnacly abutment into a crack. There he turned and hauled in the rope.

'It's a good place for landing,' said Donnie, 'but not for getting off.'

Thus encouraged, the Apprentice and I, having passed the kit over on the rope, followed the Doctor; gripping tight, we avoided complete immersion.

Donnie swivelled away, raised an arm, and vanished into a rush-hour of grey shoulders. He was to return next morning. The weather was forecast fair.

Technically, the climb was Mild Severe, but the exposure, the guano, the smell and the feathers — horrible. Am Bodach rocked like the boat and squawked like a poultry farm. The Doctor employed an extended length of car aerial to prod baby fulmars in the belly from a safe distance; they vented their horrid oil before he reached them. Some of it fell on us. I held my own stomach down. Guillemots, razorbills, gulls of all dimensions packed this riotous high-rise, balconies screaming and flapping, corridors trundling débris. How could *we* disturb them?

The Doctor led the last pitch. He stood on the summit in the sun — we had come up the north, the only possible, side — and exulted. To help his drying, he climbed down south a little, into a sentry box; and took off his clothes. They fluttered in the wind on a length of line, to the indignation of our fellow-tenants, who dived about them and marked their displeasure. The Apprentice and I relaxed on the summit, a sloping desk lid, batting the occasional too-inquisitive fowl. The Doctor had raised a small cairn — half a dozen stones or so — at the base of the lid. We piled more rocks and stones on to the Doctor's embryo and by the end of the afternoon had built a massive structure, proof obvious to all the coast of our success.

The sun cooled; the Doctor was putting on his clothes. We slid down to his niche. Warm. He was brisk and contented. Dry now. 'Wish my wallet was, but I didn't risk bringing it down here. Left it at the top for safety, under some stones. Hope you haven't knocked 'em off . . .'

It was dark before we had rebuilt our cairn, a shadow of its former self. Hard words had been said. But the sunset restored us.

We roped down to the platform selected for the bivouac; set up our bags and brewed a reasonable meal. We beat off skin-headed urchins and irresponsible parents. Eggshells, and worse, were dropped on our heads. We were pecked, intimately, during the night.

We woke to the roar of wind and wave. Settled weather . . .

Rain lashed us all that day. The coast was hidden in cloud and spume. The boat? We laughed hollowly. Birds wrung themselves dry above us.

The next night was calmer, but for birds; the next day quite calm. But no sign of boat. We had eaten most of our food, and eyed the birds with more personal interest. We climbed the summit, and shouted. We drank chicken soup from the rain puddles. Small clouds sailed above us, white wings beneath us. Donnie can act strange . . . Or perhaps dirt had finally stuck in the carburettor . . .

Almost evening. And then a boat. Two boats, fast launches. We roped down to the landing slab. The launches came closer. They were huge. One was grey, with numbers and letters on it — U.S. NAVY; the other was darker, and labelled POLICE. Lord . . .

Both were too clumsy to get very close. Both addressed us with loudhailers, simultaneously. Breaking waves drowned the confusion. They hailed at each other. They almost collided. We were pleased to see a fist shaken, not at us.

A helicopter appeared. U.S. NAVY.

This was becoming serious. Perhaps Am Bodach was somebody's Secret Weapon; a lot of money at stake somewhere.

The police launch — and was it Edie and Jim in there with them? — was smaller, and nosed nearer; its opponent retired and loud-hailed vigorously, with aerial support. Then it disappeared behind the stack. The police drew still closer in — and then faltered, swung round, and vanished behind the stack also. The helicopter cried in distress and it too fluttered behind the stack. Nobody came back.

The Apprentice rattled up and traversed south. He called to us. He was leaping about dangerously. We struggled after him. In the evening sun, a police launch tended a slowly-disappearing one-end-up unsinkable U.S. Navy launch, the water marmaladed with orange jackets. Above, a bereaved helicopter wrung its blades, beating wingless and helpless, dangling ineffectual wires.

The Bodach long ago had a crony to the south, centuries gone to his rest; but his boots, so to speak, remained, and at low tide (as now) poked up to the surface.

We did not wish our rescuers ill, but their concentrated approach would now be diluted. Yet, another night on the Bodach? We turned and longed at the coast.   Nothing.   At the sea.   Nothing.   Below, at the landing place.   Lord!

A small boat.   Donnie.

We clattered down, slithered over slabs, tossed rucksacks and ropes and jumped ecstatically but accurately into the sputtering craft. Donnie swung her round, revved up, and off we went.

'I was delayed,' he said, puffing.

No other conversation was possible in the noise. We beached and hauled up the boat. Two police officers came down to meet us; one senior, red and sauntering, the other pale and earnest. Inspector Macleod introduced himself. 'Better weather the day.' Och, he just had a few statements to take. Perhaps we could go up to the house together. The tents? Och, the tents would be safe. Donnie stayed, poking under his hatches.

Round Donnie's austere table, we learnt a little of the confusion. The Inspector pushed back his cap; his neck and grizzly hair sweated across his collar. The constable leant intensely at a notebook on his knee. Mr Twite had been worried about his birds, and had telephoned the police. The police had tried to contact Donnie, but Donnie was away.

'The Yanks had got him.'

Yanks had got him? Yes, he was being questioned by the United States Authorities across the fence. The Inspector jerked his thumb. Donnie was always being questioned by the United States Authorities across the fence. 'They think he's a spy,' chuckled the Inspector. 'What, Russian?' we asked, agape. 'Aye — or English . . . ' was the answer, 'but he's probably paid by the C.I.A. to see what they're up to.' Certainly, Donnie's other room, through the half-open door, bristled with wires and dials. 'He was a radio operator in the Merchant Navy,' explained the Inspector, 'and still likes tinkering with the wavebands.' He chortled wheezily. 'They thought he was mebbe landing agents on Am Bodach . . . they saw signals flying' (the Doctor's washing?). More chortling. 'Mind ye, my opinion is that Jim Twite's the Fifth Man — no doubt whatever.' Wheeze. The lack of whisky in the house made itself almost audible. Donnie came in and sat amongst us. The Inspector set to business.

'Well, then, *did* ye land at all?' The assistant's pencil was poised, recorders were no doubt buzzing in ample blue pockets.

Yes, we did.

'Did ye *intend* to land, Mr McIsaac?' — question to Donnie. He answered calmly that no, *he* did not.

'Then how was it these gentlemen found themselves on the top of Am Bodach, frightening the birdies and the U.S. Navy?'

Donnie impassively recounted how the Doctor had fallen into the water while we were admiring Am Bodach. How he struggled to the rock and climbed it for safety. How we two had joined him for further security. 'Is one man by himself in a dangerous position on rocks like those?' the Inspector asked us. We assented, vigorously.

'Then, Mr McIsaac, why did you not stay and take them off again immediately?'

'I had dirt in the carburettor; and I went back to the shore. And then the weather was bad; and I had — Americans.' All true. The Inspector nodded. Statements were concluded and signed. We had had no wish to disturb the various species, subspecies or genera of Aves covered by the Order, or harm the fledglings. 'Wouldn't hurt a hair of their heads,' protested the Doctor, somewhat unzoologically. Notebooks were folded, recorders (probably) switched off. The Inspector stood up.   'You'll likely hear nothing more from us.'   We went to pack up the tents. The Apprentice came rushing back.

'There's a *sentry* outside the tents!'

So there was. An at-ease very uneasy very tall U.S. Marine in full combat dress with rifle and bayonet, gazing awkwardly westward towards an invisible Old Glory.

'Aye, he's on guard. But take down yer tents. He canna stop ye. We're no in the *Area* here.' The Inspector forcefully reassured the still Caledonian earth with the square toe of his boot.

We packed the tents and left the sentry protecting the hard-pressed silverweed. No word was exchanged, but he appeared to be having difficulties with his candy. We went back into Donnie's house. The Inspector twiddled his walkie-talkie, glanced at his assistant. 'Mrs Vortoff's found a man watching her caravan again. Away and check up, Constable. I'll join you at the station.'   Having cleared the room, the Inspector relaxed and recounted amusing tales of life in the neighbourhood — catfights among the officers' wives, revolt and bribery in the native quarters. A flask had appeared. We all quaffed except Donnie, who sat a little aside, puffing his pipe. At length he rose and washed up the glasses. We followed the Inspector to his car. A lift along the road — behind the fence — to our car?'   'Safe?'   'Och, they'll no touch you.'

We were not so sure. We were less sure when we met a well-sprung and epauletted staff car, freshly serviced from the Pentagon. We stopped and were introduced to Major Altenheimer, of the U.S. Marines. Just then, the Inspector's radio crackled loudly. He listened and swore. 'There does seem to be a man watching Mrs Vortoff,' he said 'poor felly! I'll have to go there right away. The Major — ' some hurried conversation — 'the Major's going your direction, he'll take you.'

We meekly entered the staff car. The Major hailed from

Denver, Colorado, and the Doctor soon had him happily back in radiant heat and electrical sun. But the Major had only driven up to Routt National Forest, never climbed Mount Dirkel or Dome Peak, and the Doctor's merciless description of these mountains, and of buttes, canyons and sagebush horizons brought tears to his eyes. He jerked inexpressibly at the dour evening bog outside. 'I guess you *like* this sort of thing but . . . Jeeze . . . '

Shortly after, we passed lights on our left.

'Look, why don't we go down eat in the mess? You guys must be starving.' We were. 'Sure, I'll get you in.' We had no choice, anyway.

In the mess we were plied with food, drink and eager young officers. All were desperately homesick — for Maine, for Vermont, Tennessee, Washington State . . . The Doctor had been to most of these places, and laid it on thick. The Apprentice had spent ten days at Yosemite, and found an assault lieutenant who knew every route on El Capitan . . . It was a bewildering night, littered with lone stars from Texas and inextricable trails from New England, yarns from Mount McKinley to Old Smoky, Katahdin to Crater Lake. But never a word on Am Bodach or a navy launch.

We explored most of that marvellous country, and then the Doctor moved them further east to the rival Elysium and enthralled them with tales of convivial alpinism in the Caucasus and ski-touring in the Urals. They listened with shocked delight, as schoolgirls to rude stories. They peered behind furtively. He almost convinced them that the Laws of Gravity were applied more or less impartially throughout Russia.

Gorged with hospitality, we staggered to the offered beds. 'Why, you can't go back to an empty car . . . ' But we demurred at pyjamas, and collapsed in our clothes.

The next day after breakfast (no Major) we were respectfully chauffeured to the Doctor's old Mercedes. But the Doctor had been booked, for two bald back tyres. The pale young constable attended, pencil and radio. The victim protested vigorously, produced calipers and micrometer and might possibly have proved his point in the High Court. But the walkie-talkie crackled, Am Bodach winked, and it was easier to compromise and buy two new tyres and have them fitted, at fearful cost, by the garage opposite. Then — the crackle assured him — the charge need not go forward: och, yes, the tread might be enough just *now*, but not by the time he'd reach Edinburgh, and he might be — stopped — on the way. Of course. He paid the bill. No sign of the Inspector. But the garage proprietor turned out to be his brother; and would convey our greetings.

We had suffered memorable experiences, but thought it best not to publish an account of the route; still, my companions had taken photographs enough to loosen the floor of any lecture room.

A fortnight later the Apprentice burst into the back bar of Daddy McKay's, brandishing a box of slides. He spilled them on to the liquid table — blank, blank, all of them. All those wonderful shots of Am Bodach, the Doctor's washing, the sinking launch . . . He had been sent, by Kodak as consolation, a little booklet on *'Do's and Don'ts for Beginners'* or suchlike. He cursed and swore.

'X-rays,' said the Doctor, pleasantly.

We remembered our rucksacks in the corner of the bedroom at the mess . . .

'Don't worry, mine are all right,' said the Doctor, 'we'll duplicate 'em. Some excellent ones. I took out the film in the tent before we left; kept the spool in my pocket. Best thing. And always sleep in your clothes.'

We were aghast.

He tipped back his glass.

'Learned that in Russia,' he said.